Principles and Application of

ENVIRONMENTAL IMPACT ASSESSMENT (EIA)

Benard A. Omoyeni

FOREWORD: PROF. ADEOFUN OLABINJO

Published in Nigeria by
McORNELS VENTURES
121, Okota Road, by Cele B/Stop, Lagos.
Tel: +234 (0) 8169848450, +234 (0)8123076068
E-mail:ornelsmail@gmail.com

For enquiries call:
+234 (0) 8033677288
Email:bennydotun@gmail.com

DEDICATION

The book is dedicated to the glory of God and the benefit of nature to mankind.

ACKNOWLEDGMENTS

I deeply appreciate the Almighty God for the inspiration of the Holy Spirit that enabled me to generate the idea and energy to write and prepare this book for publication. To God be all the glory for making this book a reality.

I am forever indebted to my parents, Chief Julius and Mrs Regina Omoyeni for my upbringing and training. The values of diligence, integrity, resilience and goodwill they imbued in me have made me become a total man that I am today.

I am eternally grateful to my Spiritual father, pastor, mentor and role model, Bishop David Oyedepo for his insightful and impactful teachings deeply rooted in the word of God, which have lightened me and made my life a wonder to behold.

I appreciate my teachers who thought me the fundamentals of environmental science and management in my undergraduate years at the Federal University of Technology, Akure and my Post graduate days at the University of Maiduguri, University of Agriculture, Abeokuta and University of Ibadan respectively. Notable of mention among many of my teachers are Dr. Demola Borode, Prof. A. M Balogun, Prof. Emmanuel Fasakin, Prof. (Mrs.) Yemisi Adeparusi, Prof. Dayo Agbelusi, Dr. D. H. Godowoli, Dr. A.Dlakwa, Prof. Clement Adeofun, Prof C. Omoniyi, Prof W. Alagbeleye, Prof. Seyi Fabiyi, Pro. Bola Ayeni and Prof. S. Abumere of blessed memory.

I sincerely appreciate the suppor ... ...is
gracious acceptance to write the ... ...is
demanding schedule as the Dean of the College of E........ ...al
Resources Management, University of Agriculture, Abeokuta. I say
thank you Sir.

I recall with nostalgic feelings and sense of indebtedness to Dr.
Aminu Raji for the opportunity he gave me on research endeavours
and leadership functions during my days at the Federal College of
Freshwater Fisheries Technology, Baga, Maiduguri.

My gratitude also goes to Otunba Amid Adekunle for his roles in my
exposure to the corporate world of environmental management
and regulatory advocacy.

I will always appreciate my sister, Mrs Rosemary Akindele for her
leadership and sacrifice in providing the broad shoulder I leaned
on to advance my education during my undergraduate days. I
acknowledge the support and goodwill of my younger siblings in
challenging me to provide leadership thereby making me
responsible as their role model. Thanks to Emmanuel, Joseph,
Charles, Patrick, Bonaventure Omoyeni and Opeyemi Ogunsuyi
(Mrs.) for their goodwill and prayers.

I am blessed with great uncles and cousins who have provided
strong support for me to stand tall among my peers. Worthy of
mention are Pastor Jide Omoyeni, Pastor Sola Ologun, Mr.

Ogoluwa Omoyeni, Dr. Remi Ajakaiye, AIG Ade Ajakaiye (Rtd.) and Navy Comdr Dele Orimolade.

I appreciate the many good people God has brought my way to inspire, motivate, support and help me achieve my dreams all along. My very good friends Pastor Ademola Ajisola, Vincent Shaba, Olaide Oladunjoye, Vincent Akerele, Dr, Olusegun Emiju and Pastor Segun Oyemakinde are worthy to be appreciated.

I appreciate the painstaking effort of Mrs. Ijeoma AniKelechi in the typing of the manuscript of this book. The effort of Mr. Ani Kelechi Johnmary of the Federal University Ndufu-Alike, Ikwo, Ebonyi State in proof reading this book is sincerely appreciated.

Finally, my profound and ultimate thanks go to my soul mate, my wife and priceless jewel, Mrs. Uzoma Maryanne Omoyeni for her support, love and understanding. Thanks for believing in me and always being there giving me and our wonderful children; Newdawn, Delight and Excel the very best as wife and mother. You are in indeed a virtuous woman whose price is far above rubies!

CONTENTS

FORWARD

The various environmental problems arising from the impact of human activities on the environment are manifestations of the disharmony between development and environment, and they threaten to destroy the basis of development itself. The natural environment is man's life support system that must be wisely utilized and protected to ensure sustainability.

Environmental Impact assessment (E.I.A) is designed to assess in advance the likely impact of a development project on the environment before such project is implemented and it is now being adopted all over the world as an instrument of public policy in deciding the type and locations of development projects to be executed. It is therefore imperative to study and understand the principles and application of this important environmental concept such that it can be used as a veritable tool for sustainable environmental management.

The book covered the substantive and contemporary issues involved in E. I. A. In particular the book highlighted key concepts, methodologies, practical approaches and more importantly the role of stakeholder engagement and public consultation in a typical E. I. A study. It is remarkable to note that the quality of the book in terms of depth and richness of contents, scholarly presentation and topics covered are quite high.

This book will no doubt help students both undergraduates and post graduates to acquire the basic theoretical knowledge and practical applications needed to solve environmental problems. In particular the book will guide environmental practitioners, consultants and scientist on how E. I. A can be used as a tool for decision making in solving major environmental problems resulting from development project/activities. Teachers of environmental sciences in Nigerian Universities, Polytechnics and colleges of Education will also find the book very useful.

This book is the result of the author's accumulated experience build on his research and practical exposures that have spammed over one and half decade.

Prof. Adeofun Olabinjo
Dean, College of Environmental Resources Management.
Federal University of Agriculture,
Abeokuta, Nigeria.

PREFACE

The phrase Environmental Impact Assessment (EIA), which is derived from section 102(2) of the United States National Environmental Policy Act (NEPA), 1969 has become a widely accepted tool for decision making in project development and execution. The EIA extrapolates from scientific knowledge to assess the consequences of human intervention on nature and environment to ensure that there is a balance between development and environment.

The challenges of sustainable development have taken center stage as one of the most important issues facing humanity in the twenty first century. Achieving economic growth and securing higher standards of living should not be at the expense of the environment, this is because the environment is the foundation upon which existence of all forms of life depends as well as remains the life support system for human continuity.

The realities of environmental degradation, climate change and associated effects can no longer be denied, global warming issues have generated high global attention and the need to urgently entrench the principles of sustainable development, and pragmatically address the root causes of global warming and climate change.

Consequently, EIA has proven to be a key instrument that can be used in decisions that promotes sustainable growth and development. Nevertheless, an EIA remains a cosmetic tool if the principles and applications are not well understood. The understanding of the EIA process and its application provides the platform for its effective use as tool for environmental management and sustainable development.

The purpose of this book is to present a simplified and practical approach that will enhance the quality of understanding of the principles and application of EIA through the interpretation of the fundamental requirements of Environmental Impact of Assessment. This book is written to boost the body of knowledge on EIA with the intent to offer easy-to-use guidance for undergraduate and postgraduate students of environmental studies, environment practitioners, consultants and corporate organizations on the subject of EIA.

There are eight chapters in this book. Chapter one presents the background information on the subject of EIA, defining key concepts of the subject, which is meant to prepare the readers for good understanding of the subject as they explore the pages of the book which is loaded with practical guides on application of EIA

Chapter two discuses the purpose, scope and objectives of EIA, EIA mandatory activities, tools and resources required for EIA. Chapter three details the step by step procedures of undertaking EIA for projects as well as activities required in line with regulatory requirements and global best practices. Chapter four presents information on the methodologies for environmental characterization with practical guidance on field data gathering, laboratory analysis and data interpretation.

Chapter five on its part presents the impact assessment methodologies and easy to use guidance on project impact identification, assessment and prediction towards understanding the basic elements and steps used in identifying and assessing project impacts that is realistic and verifiable. Chapter six presents the guidance on developing cost effective impact mitigation measures that will be practicable and effective in mitigating or ameliorating projects environmental and socio-economic impacts.

Chapter seven discusses the elements of an Environmental Management Plan (EMP) and the requirements for implementing the EMP so as to derive the values it adds to EIA as a management tool for ensuring project sound environmental performance. Chapter eight presents stakeholders consultation and engagement as a critical activity of the EIA process and its relevance in defining the quality of the EIA and project acceptability by a network of stakeholders.

Although the book is not exhaustive on the subject of EIA, it provides useful guidance that simplifies the subject based on the author's over one and half decade hands on experience built on his research and academic prowess. It is the author's expectation that this book will provide the template for quality EIA development and application for environment-lovers across the globe, thereby promoting the achievement of the principles of sustainable development.

Chapter One

CONCEPT OF ENVIRONMENTAL IMPACT ASSESSMENT

This chapter presents the background information on the subject of EIA, defining key concepts of the subject, which is meant to prepare the readers for good understanding of the subject as they explore the pages of the book which is loaded with practical guides on application of EIA

The contemporary journey towards environmental policy and acts started in response to two major disasters that resulted in an unprecedented damages to aquatic and marine life in England and United States of America, the National Environmental Policy Acts (NEPA) passed in 1969 creates the Council on Environmental Quality (CEQ), which provides the requirement for analysis of the environmental impact of major federal actions significantly affecting the quality of the human environment.

The England incident of 1967 that involved the disintegration of "Torey Canyon," an oil tanker which was loaded with some 120 tons of oil and the California incident of 1969 resulting from accidental striking of oil by an offshore drilling rig that caused large spillages, which in turn led to colossal damages to aquatic and marine life underscored the importance of assessing the consequences of a given action on the environment. This led to the setting up of the environmental policy organization by the United States Government. The body is saddled with advising the U.S Congress on matters concerning the environment, especially as they relate to its planning, aesthetics, design and protection among others.

The term Environmental Impact Assessment (EIA) and Environmental Impact Statement (EIS) were first used officially in the National Environmental Policy Act (NEPA) passed in 1969 by U.S Congress, which became effective on January 1, 1970. Consequently, the attention of the world would soon be drawn to the development in the United States of America that by 1972, the United Nations (UN) sponsored a conference on human environment in Stockholm, Sweden leading to the establishment of governing council for environment programme known as the United Nations Environmental Programme (UNEP). Since its inception, it has provided guidance on the environmental assessment of development proposal and supported research on environmental issues. The World Environment Conference also drew world attention to the inextricable links between development and the environment.

The Center for Environmental Management and Planning (CEMP) established in Aberdeen in 1972 has organized several annual international seminars on environmental assessment and management sponsored by the World Health Organization (WHO) and United Nations Development Programme (UNDP). In February 1974, UNEP and UNESCO co-sponsored a workshop organized by the Scientific Committee on Problems of the Environment (SCOPE).The workshop that was held in Victoria Harbor, Canada was to synthesize inter-state EIA methods and practices. Participants were drawn from diverse disciplines and the outcome was the publication of SCOPE Environmental Impact Assessment: Principles and Procedures.

Since 1975, many countries have continued to adopt EIA process in decision making as well as project development and execution. However, concerns about environmental impacts of development or operation vary from country to country. The differences in political and institutional framework of the nations of the world are major factors influencing the degree of commitment to the principles of EIA and its application as a tool for decision making.

1.1   Historical Background of EIA

The United States of America (USA) was the first country to develop a system of Environmental Impact Assessment (EIA). When Silent Spring written by Rachel Carson was published in 1962, social awareness to environmental issues in the US had reached high proportions and grew as very intense movements at the latter half of 1960s particularly with the occurrence of California and Torey Canyon incidents. With these social backgrounds, the National Environmental Policy Act (1969) of the United States of America (NEPA) was constituted and for the first time, EIA policy requiring environmental consideration in large scale projects was enforced as legislation. The influence of NEPA in which the concept of EIA system has its bedrock was extended beyond the US and that provoked the introduction of EIA policy in many countries in Europe and Asia. Following the US initiative, several countries began to come-up with EIA systems. For instance Australia (1974), Thailand (1975), France (1976), Philippines (1978), Israel (1981), Pakistan (1983) and Nigeria(1992).

However, it should be noted that EIA has evolved significantly over the past 30 years, driven by improvements in laws, procedures and methodology. Today, EIA is applied in more than 100 countries by governments, development banks and most international Aid agencies. The evolution of EIA can be divided into 4 overlapping phases which include:

Introduction and Early Development Phase (1969 -1975) – During this period, the mandate and foundations of EIA was established in the USA and was then adopted by a few other countries (e.g. Australia, Canada and New Zealand). The basic concept, procedure and methodology still apply.

Increasing Scope and Sophistication Phase (Mid 1970's to early 1980's) – This period was characterized by more advanced techniques, issuance of guidance on process implementation, consideration of social impacts and adoption by more countries including the developing nations of China, Thailand and the Philippines.

Process Strengthening and Integration Phase (Early 1980's to early 1990's) – This era witnessed the review of EIA practice and experience; updates of scientific and institutional frameworks of EIA; coordination of EIA with other processes; consideration of cumulative effects, ecosystem-level changes, monitoring and other follow-up mechanisms. Many more countries adopted EIA during this period and the European Community and the World Bank respectively established national and international lending requirements.

Strategic and Sustainability Orientation Phase (Early 1990's to date) – The current phase of EIA evolution has entailed the incorporation of EIA aspects in international agreements; increase in international training; capacity building and networking activities; development of Strategic Environmental Assessments (SEA) of policies and plans as well as the inclusion of sustainability concepts and criteria in EIA and SEA practice. EIA is currently applied in all OECD countries and large numbers of developing and transitional countries including Nigeria.

1.2 EIA Practices around the World
1.2.1 EUROPEAN UNION (EU)

The EIA Directive on Environmental Impact Assessment of project effects was first introduced in 1985 and amended in 1997 (Watson, M, 2003). The directive was amended again in 2003 following the 1998 signature of the Aarhus Convention on Public Participation in environmental matters. The EIA directive established a mix of mandatory and discretionary procedures for assessing environmental impacts under the EU directive, which shows that

EIA must provide certain information for compliance. There are seven key areas that are required, they include:

1. Description of the project: Description of key components i.e. construction operation and decommissioning. For each of the components, lists all of the sources of environmental disturbance.

2. Alternatives that have been considered for the project/activity.

3. Description of the environment (list of all aspects of the environment that may be affected by the development e.g. population, fauna, flora, air, soil, water, landscape, cultural heritage etc and this section is best carried-out with the help of local experts.

4. Description of the significant effects on the environment by examination of potential interaction between project activities and the environment.

5. Mitigation: This is where the EIA is most useful in developing measures to reduce or avoid the significant effects.

6. Non-technical Summary: A summary that does not include jargons that can be understood by informed lay-person because the EIA will be in the public domain and be used in decision making process.

7. Lack of Know-how/ Technical Difficulties. This section is to advise on any area of weakness in knowledge so it can be used to focus on areas of future research.

1.2.2 UNITED KINGDOM (UK)

When EIA was first introduced into the UK, there was widespread complacency over the degree to which it would change the planning process. This complacency prevailed for several years and was reinforced by decisions in the UK courts that were very relaxed about the requirement to comply with the EIA directive.

In the UK, the EIA procedures are not formalized in one legislation as in the U.S and some other countries, rather the impact of proposed developments are considered under a wide range of procedures which can be categorized into planning controls and pollution controls.

Local government covers administration of regional land use programs and development control, which is carried-out by the Town and County Planning Regulations in which EIA procedures are stipulated. Approval for highways, power stations and other major infrastructure projects however, is issued by the national government in accordance with relevant laws, for example, the Highways Act or Electricity Act. EIA procedures for these projects are stipulated in the individual laws. Individual laws are made to comply with EC directives for maintaining an approval system that is used by both national and local governments. In EIA procedures the significant role local government agencies play as regional planning agencies is regulation administration and flexible cooperation between agencies and project executors from the early stages of project development.

Meanwhile, the complacency on EIA implementation has largely been swept away by a series of recent court cases which have signaled a far more rigorous attitude. These cases have mainly focused on the need for EIA in a variety of circumstances. The cases provide illuminating comments on the content and quality of environmental statements and associated EIA process. Council Directive 1997/11/EC of March 3, 1997 which amended the 1985 Directive declares that Environmental Impact Assessment is a fundamental policy. Since the directive came to force there have been several studies of the quality of environmental statements. These studies have highlighted discrepancies in the quality of assessment and have identified weaknesses in project EIA procedure which include:

  a) Non-existed or weak follow-up process.
  b) The inadequate treatment of cumulative effects and other factors.
  c) Public consultation is sub-standard.
  d) Environmental impacts are understated and insufficiently mitigated.

1.2.3 UNITED STATED OF AMERICA (USA)

The National Environmental Policy Act of 1969 (NEPA), enacted in 1970, established a policy of environmental impact assessment for federal agency actions, federally funded activities or federally permitted/licensed activities that in the U. S. is termed "environmental review" or simply "the NEPA process. Under United States environmental law an Environmental Assessment (EA) is compiled to determine the need for an Environmental Impact Statement (EIS). In the U.S , EIA is referred to as EIS, Federal or federalized actions expected to subject or be subject to significant environmental impacts will publish a Notice of Intent to Prepare an EIS as soon as significance is known.. An environmental assessment (environmental analysis) is prepared pursuant to the National Environmental Policy Act to determine whether a federal action would significantly affect the environment and thus require a more detailed Environmental Impact Statement (EIS).

The certified release of an Environmental Assessment results in either a Finding of No Significant Impact (FONSI) or an EIS. EA was originally intended to be a simple document used in relatively rare instances where an agency was not sure if the potential significance of an action would be sufficient to trigger preparation of an EIS. but today, because EISs are so much longer and complicated to prepare, federal agencies are going to great effort to avoid preparing EISs by using EAs, even in cases where the use of EAs may be inappropriate. The ratio of EAs that are being issued compared to EISs is about 100 to 1 (Eccleston and Peyton 2012)

The purpose of NEPA process is to ensure that decision makers are fully informed of the environmental aspects and consequences of their policy objective(s) prior to making final decision.

Usually, an agency will release a Draft on Environmental Impact Statement (DEIS) for comment. Interested parties and the general public will have the opportunity to comment on the draft, after which the agency will approve the Final Environmental Impact Statement (FEIS). Occasionally, the agency will later release a Supplemental Environmental Impact Statement (SEIS) especially if the environmental conditions suddenly change after the issuance of FEIS.

The adequacy of an EIS can be challenged in court. Major proposed projects have been blocked because of an agency's failure to prepare acceptable EIS. A prominent case involved the Sierra Club suing the Nevada Department of Transportation over its denial of Sierra Club's request to issue supplementary EIS addressing air emissions of particulate matter and hazardous air pollutants in the case of widening US highway 95 through Las Vegas. The case reached the 9th circuit court of the United States which led to construction on the highway being halted until the court's final decision. Paradoxically, the case was settled prior to the court's final decision (http://elr.info/litigation)

Several US state government have adopted "little NEPA" i.e. state laws imposing EIS requirements for particular state actions and some of those states refer to the required environmental impact studies as Environmental Impact Reports or Environmental Impact Assessments (David Sive et.al 2005). For example, the California Environmental Quality Act (CEQA) requires an Environmental Impact Report (EIR) for development activities. Typical EIA for a major project in the USA takes one to two years.

1.2.4 CHINA

Environmental Impact Assessment Law in China is among the major statues that have evolved since the passage of the draft Environmental Protection Law in 1979. It is stipulated in the "Environmental Protection Law (pilot phase, 1979) that all construction related projects must implement EIA. EIA procedures were clearly defined in the Basic Construction Items Environmental Preservation Management Law established in 1981.The main features of the administrative systems in China include the fact that no provisions are made for public participation, the EIA work is carried out by qualified executive EIA organizations. Filling out of simple EIS Forms is sufficient for small scale projects.

The Environmental Impact Assessment Law (EIA Law) requires an Environmental Impact Assessment to be completed prior to project construction. However, if a developer completely ignores this requirement and builds a project without submitting an Environmental Impact Statement, the only penalty is that the Environmental Protection Bureau (EPB) may require the developer to do a make-up environmental assessment. If the developer does not complete this make-up assessment within the designated time only then is the EPB authorized to fine the developer, even so, the possible fine is capped at a maximum of about US $25,000; a fraction of the overall cost of most major projects. This indicates a lack of stringent enforcement (Wang A. 2007).

The allowance for "make-up" environmental assessments creates a loophole around the fundamental reason for environmental impact assessment (i.e., to build environmental considerations into the development of projects and plans before they are completed). Chinese environmental officials and scholars are well-aware of these weaknesses in the law and openly acknowledge that they are the result of compromises in the legislative process and concerns about limiting economic growth, this has resulted in a significant percentage of projects not completing legally required environmental impact assessment prior to construction (Wang, A 2007)

Meanwhile, China's State Environmental Protection Administration (SEPA) used the legislation to halt 30 projects in 2004 including three hydro-power plants under the three Gorges Project Company, Although one month later most of the 30 halted projects resumed their construction, reportedly having passed the environmental assessment, the fact that these key projects' construction was ever suspended was noticeable but considering the requirement, for addressing EIA issues, one month is grossly inadequate to the suspension of the projects.

A joint investigation by SEPA and Ministry of Land Resources in 2004 showed that 30 to 40 percent of mining construction projects went through the procedure of environmental impact assessment as required while in some areas only 6 to 7 percent did so, this partly explains why China has witnessed so many mining incidents in recent years.

The decades of rapid industrialization in the face of weak environmental impact assessment process have created enormous environmental challenges in China. The problems are, by now, well known. Seventeen of the 25 most polluted cities in the world can be found in China. The rate of China's environmental laws and regulations that are actually enforced is estimated to be barely 10 percent (Wang, A 2007)

1.2.5 Hong Kong

The effort to formulate a set of administrative EIA procedures for public and private sector projects, with regard to developmental pressures and social characteristics started in 1979. The application of the EIA process by pioneers in the then Environmental Protection Agency resulted in the integration of environmental considerations into the site selection, design, construction and operation of major development projects such as a new coal-fired 1,700MW power station, the development of Tin ShuiWai new town and Chek Lap Kok airport. During this period, a limited number (23 in total) of EIAs were completed.

In 1985, the emphasis on the integration of environmental factors into the land use planning process led to the formation of a set of environmental standards and guidelines incorporated into the Hong Kong Planning and Standards Guidelines. Shortly afterwards, the EIA process in Hong Kong developed from an ad hoc requirement imposed on a small number of government and private infrastructure projects, to a set of systematic administrative procedures to be followed by proponents of all major or environmentally significant development projects (private and public) in Hong Kong.

The Hong Kong Government issued in 1986 an internal directive entitled 'Environmental Review of Major Development Projects', which set out the screening process and EIA requirements for public works. The administrative EIA procedures were subsequently laid down in two other documents. During this period, a total of about 80 EIA's were completed, covering a wide range of projects such as roads, sewage treatment works, major residential developments and waste disposal facilities. During the 1990s, the number of EIA's continued to increase significantly. From 1992 to 1994, a total of 239 EIA's were completed or ongoing, compared to only 80 EIAs during the previous six-year period. A strong demand was voiced from the public, district boards, the Legislative Council and other government advisory bodies for a more thorough consideration of environmental impacts of development projects before the commencement of construction. The EIA process underwent three major developments during this period. First, the process was formally stated as a planning tool for decision-makers, which included a conflict resolution mechanism to resolve disagreements. Second, a new requirement was added to make EIA reports available to the public for open inspection. Third, a formal system of environmental monitoring and auditing was introduced to track the actual performance of projects.

Since the 1990s, the Environmental Protection Department has contributed to a number of strategic planning studies, including the Territorial Development Strategy Review. In his policy address in October 1992, the Governor of Hong Kong introduced a new requirement for EIAs to be included in study papers submitted to the Executive Council. Because of this initiative, policy submissions to the Executive Council must now include environmental implications and sections to assist in better decision-making. Likewise, environmental implications sections have become a prerequisite for all requests by public sector projects for funding approval that are considered by the Public Works Sub-Committee of the Legislative Council's Finance Committee. 'Environmental Implication' statements have since been included in study papers seeking funding and policy approval.

The Environmental Impact Assessment Bill was introduced for its first reading in the Legislative Council on 31 January 1996 and was debated. The EIA Ordinance was subsequently enacted on 4 February 1997 and its two subsidiary regulations on the appeal board and application fees were approved by the Provisional Legislative Council in June and November 1997 respectively. The Ordinance came into operation on 1 April 1998. For the first time in Hong Kong, environmental impact assessments became mandatory for designated projects. It is now an offense to construct, operate or decommission a designated project listed in Schedule II of the EIA Ordinance without an environmental permit or contrary to the conditions, if any, set out in the permit.

1.2.6 INDIA

Environmental action formally started with the participation of India in the UN conference on human environment in Stockholm in 1972. A National Committee on Environmental Planning and Coordination (NCEPC) was established to be the apex body in the department of science and technology. The term environment figured for the first time in India's fourth year plan (1969-1974) which recorded that harmonious development is possible only on the basis of a comprehensive appraisal of environmental issues.

The Tiwari committee on review of legislative and administrative measures in its report in 1980 recommended the creation of a department of environment as a nodal agency to ensure cation in environmental impact protection and to carry out environment impact studies of proposed development projects and to have administrative responsibility for pollution monitoring and control. The department metamorphosed into the Ministry of Environment and Forest with the Prime Minister holding its charge. Since its inception, the department under the ministry has issued various guidelines on EIA for various projects. Meanwhile, legal and legislative instruments of enforcement are weak and this no doubt affects compliance with guidelines on EIA processes and application in that country.

1.2.7 AUSTRALIA

The history of EIA in Australia could be linked to the enactment of the U.S. National Environment Policy Act (NEPA) in 1969, which made the preparation of environmental impact statements a requirement. Meanwhile, EIA procedures were introduced at a State Level prior to that of the Commonwealth (Federal), with a majority of the states having divergent views to the Commonwealth . EIA provisions at the federal level are contained within the Environmental Protection and Biodiversity Conservation Act (EPBC) 1999.

At the state level, each jurisdiction has EIA provisions typically contained in land use planning law, for example in New South Wales, EIA is performed under either part 3A, part 4 or part 5 of the Environmental Planning and Assessment Act (1979) depending on the type of development. An important point to note is that this Commonwealth Act does not affect the validity of the States and Territories environmental and development assessments and approvals; rather the EPBC runs as a parallel to the State/Territory Systems Elliott, M. & Thomas, I. (2009) The overlap between federal and state requirements is addressed through bilateral agreements as provided for in the EPBC Act.

The EPBC Act provides a legal framework to protect and manage nationally and internationally important flora, fauna, ecological communities and heritage places-defined in the EPBC Act as matters of 'national environmental significance

The EPBC Act comes into play when a person (a 'proponent') wants an action (often called a 'proposal' or 'project') assessed for environmental impacts under the EPBC Act, he or she must refer the project to the Department of Environment, Water, Heritage and the Arts (Australia). This 'referral' is then released to the public, as well as relevant state, territory and Commonwealth ministers, for comment on whether the project is likely to have a significant impact on matters of national environmental significance

1.2.8 NEW ZEALAND

In New Zealand, EIA is usually referred to as Assessment of Environmental Effects (AEE). The first use of EIA's in that country dates back to a cabinet minutes passed in 1974, which was called

Environmental Procedure and Enhancement Procedures. This has no legal force and only related to the activities of government departments. When the Resources Management Act was passed in 1991, an EIA was required as part of a resource consent application.

1.2.9 SRI LANKA

In Sri Lanka, the National Environmental Acts was amended in 1988 to provide for regulations pertaining to environmental impact assessment. The Central Environmental Authority is responsible for guidelines, project selection, and coordination of various project approving authorities related to EIA. The procedures include provisions for public hearings, public announcement of approvals, and appeals against unsuccessful projects.

The importance of Environmental Impact Assessment as an effective tool for the purpose of integrating environmental considerations with development planning is highly recognized in Sri Lanka. The application of this technique is considered as a means of ensuring that the likely effects of new development projects on the environment are fully understood and taken into account before development is allowed to proceed. The importance of this management tool to foresee potential environmental impacts and problems caused by proposed projects and its use as a means to make project more suitable to the environment are highly appreciated.

1.2.10 NIGERIA

The new found awareness on environmental quality especially following the Koko toxic waste incident of 1988 led to the establishment of the Federal Environmental Protection Agency (FEPA) by Decree 58 of 1988, charged with the responsibility for the protection and development of the environment, and biodiversity, conservation and sustainable development of Nigeria natural resources in general; including policy initiation in relation to environmental research and technology. In 1989 FEPA's responsibilities were translated into the National Policy on Environment. As part of the implementation of the National Environmental Policy, interim guidelines and standards for environmental control in Nigeria were fashioned out in 1991. In 1992, the EIA Decree no 86 was promulgated to give legal muscle for the enforcement of the various policy provisions on the need for environmental impact assessment studies of both public and private sector projects. The decree made EIA mandatory for project developments that would cause some modifications in the physical, chemical, biological and socio-economic environment.

FEPA in 1999 metamorphosed to the Federal Ministry of Environment which among other things was created to discharge the functions of the defunct FEPA. The ministry has a department for environmental assessment with the mandate to coordinate and enforce compliance with the provisions of the EIA Act. In response to growing concerns for the impact of oil and oil related activities in the Nigerian oil producing areas, the Department of

Petroleum Resources in 1991 issued the Environmental Guidelines and Standards for the Petroleum Industry in Nigeria (EGASPIN) to provide the guidelines and standards for the prevention, control and management of environmental pollution. Part VIIIA of the EGASPIN which addresses standardization of environmental abatement procedures provides the guideline and requirement for Environmental Impact Assessment (EIA) for oil related activities prior to commencement of such activities.

At the state level, Environmental Protection Agencies and Ministries of Environment operating on the legal framework of the state environmental edicts and relevant federal environmental laws attempt to enforce EIA requirements project that requires the preparation of environmental impact assessment report for project prior to implementation. Nevertheless, the Federal Ministry of Environment remains the custodian of the environment and the nodal point for the coordination and enforcement of the EIA regulations in Nigeria.

Usually, draft EIA report is submitted to the Federal Ministry of Environment and the Department of Petroleum Resources (If project is oil and gas related) the Federal Ministry of Environment issues provisional EIA approvals and organizes public hearing to allow a public review of the EIA report. Upon the submission of a satisfactory final EIA report, the ministry grants final approval and issues the Environmental Impact Statement (EIS) certificate.

Much as there is high level of awareness on the requirement of EIA for development projects, there is lack of stringent enforcement mechanism particularly in the area of implementation of the post EIA impact mitigation monitoring that is a key component that can be used to measure the extent to which the EIA has achieved its objectives. EIA is perceived by most organization as regulatory obligations and not as tool for decision making.

1.3   Definition of Key Concepts

1.3.1 Environment

The term environment has a variety of definition depending on the perspective it is viewed from. Environment as defined by the World Bank (1991A) is the natural and social conditions surrounding all mankind and including future generation. Environment as an element of ecology is seen as the science of the organism in relation to other organisms of different species and to those of its own kind (Darling 1971). Environment is the sum of all external forces or influences that affect the life of organism both plant and animal.

An environment is a complex of many factors that interact not only with the organism but among themselves; the relationship between living things in an environment is the interaction of the organisms in the environment within themselves and other external forces making up the environment. The environment is thus the life support system on which life depends. EIA decree 86 (1992) defined environment as the components of the earth and it include:

- Land, water and air including all layers of the atmosphere.
- All organic and inorganic matter and living organisms, and
- The interacting natural systems that include components referred to in (a) and (b) above.

The Nigerian National Environmental Policy (1989) provides a clearer definition of environment, which makes it more applicable to EIA. It defines environment to include physical, ecosystem (biotic and abiotic elements), social, economic, cultural, aesthetic and political dimensions in their various interactions and interrelationship.

1.3.2 Ecology and Ecosystem

Ecology is the study of the relationship between living things and the environment while ecosystem is an interdependent system of living organisms and the physical environment. The ecosystem is made up of physical and biological parts both of which are so merged in their functions that individual roles cannot be ignored. The physical environment provides the energy, raw materials and living space that the biological community needs and uses for growth and maintenance. In any ecosystem, there is a machine like organization which involves production and utilization of energy and raw material from one state to the other. This complex interactions occur in aquatic and terrestrial environment, thus we have the aquatic and terrestrial ecosystem.

Terrestrial ecosystem in tropical Africa fall into three types: Forest, Savanna and Desert. These broad classifications can further be categorized into specific levels. Plant grows in an environment that lies within its tolerance range, this range is that environmental conditions within which the plant will grow. Such range is based on the physiological requirement of the plant and extent to which the abiotic or physical factor will favorably allow. Factors such as temperature, light intensity, rainfall, humidity, soil fertility, etc constitute the physical factors which are in turn vulnerable to influence of human interactions with the environment and ecosystem.

The various organisms that live grow and multiply in the aquatic ecosystem form a close association which is the level of a circle called food chain. There exist complex interactions between and among the physico-chemical and biological components of the aquatic ecosystem. Food production activities, consumption and decomposition takes place within a given tolerance limit, any alteration to the sensitive balance in the aquatic ecosystem has the potential to affect the trophic levels hence its productivity.

1.3.3 Environmental Impact

ISO 14001 defines environmental impact as any change in the environmental component whether adverse or beneficial, wholly or partially resulting from an organization's activities, product or services. According to Wathern (1988) an impact has both spatial and temporal components and can be described as the change in an environmental parameter over a specified period within a defined area resulting from a particular activity compared with the situation which would have occurred had the activity not been initiated.

Impacts result from interaction between project activities and the environmental receptors. Environmental impacts may be defined in terms of its duration, magnitude, frequency, nature, area, extent, severity etc. Similarly, impacts could be reversible or irreversible, adverse or beneficial, localized or widespread, short-term, moderate or long-term, once, intermittent or continuous.

1.3.4 Environmental Impact Assessment (EIA)

Environmental Impact Assessment (EIA) has several definitions and there is no universally accepted definition but all EIA definitions connotes same meaning and interpretations. At the centre of EIA definition is environmental protection and sustainable development.

Canter (1996) defines EIA as the systematic identification and evaluation of the potential impact (effect) of proposed project. The International Association for Impact Assessment (IAIA) defines EIA as the process of identifying, predicting, evaluating and mitigating the bio-physical, social and other relevant effects of development proposals prior to major decisions being taken and commitment made in project plans and programmes or legislative actions, relative to the physical, chemical, biological, cultural and socio- economic component of the total environment.

According to Munn (1979) EIA is an activity designed to identify, predict the impact on the bio-geophysical environment as well as on man's health and well-being, of legislative proposals, policies, programme, projects, operational procedures and to interpret and communicate about the impacts.

EIA can be defined as a systematic process for identifying, examining, analyzing, evaluating, and predicting theimpacts of planned activities or policies; involving consultation with affected stakeholders,and using the results of the analysis and consultations in planning, authorising and implementation of a project/activity (Asigbaase M, 2012)

UNEP draft guidelines prepared for assessing industrial environmental impact and evaluation criteria for the sighting of industries(1978) defined EIA as a tool to identify, predict and describe in appropriate terms as well as the pros and cons (penalties and benefits) of a proposed development.

DPR EGASPIN (2002) defines EIA as report that assesses all actions that will result in a physical, chemical, biological, cultural and social etc modification of the environment as a result of the new project development.

The FEPA (1992) in its EIA decree no 86 of 1992 defines EIA as a systematic process that provides a framework for gathering and documenting information and views regarding the environmental consequences of activities so that the importance of the effects and the scope for enhancing, modifying and mitigating them can be properly evaluated. EIA then forms an integral part of the project cycle, it provides information on the environmental, socio-economic and health effects of the proposed activities and how to manage such effects in order to ensure the protection of human life and the environment.

Again, some jurisdictions are using the term EIA broadly to include social, economic and cultural impacts, while some regard them as distinct from EIA. This often depends on the organization involved, professional judgment and institutional interpretation of the meaning of environment. Meanwhile, it is important to recognize that impacts on ecosystem, bio-physical and geochemical cycles are intimately related through complex feedback mechanism that is effectively communicated through socio-economic impacts and considerations. EIA study is carried out using a systematic, multi-disciplinary approach and should incorporate all relevant analytical disciplines to provide meaningful and factual data, information and analysis.

On a general note, EIA can be regarded as a procedure that ensures the environmental implications of project decisions are taken into account before project/development decisions are finalized. This is because the evaluation of the various environmental effects (adverse and beneficial) of a proposed action would determine the outcome of the decision that would be made on the implementation of the project.

EIA in environmental law can be described by any of the following phrases: International Equity, Polluter Pay Principle, Precautionary Principle, Public Trust Doctrine, Cradle to Grave Principle and Sustainable Development.

EIA is a policy and management tool for both planning and decision making. It assists in identifying, predicting and evaluating the foreseeable environmental consequences of proposed development projects, plans and actions. It also specifies necessary environmental protection measures that include mitigation measures to reduce adverse effects, offset unavoidable adverse effects and also measures to enhance the beneficial effects. The outcome of an EIA study would assist decision-makers and the general public to determine whether a project should be implemented and in what form.

1.3.5 Biodiversity

Biodiversity as the word states is the diversity of life, it refers to the millions of different life forms found on earth, their genetic variation, and the complex ecological interrelationships between them; as such it is the primary life support system of our planet, and a pre-condition for human survival.

Biodiversity is not only an environmental asset that determines whether or not the air we breathe and the water we drink will sustain us, as demonstrated at the 1992 Earth Summit in Rio de Janeiro, it is also a unique cultural and economic asset. Nobody knows how many different life forms or species share the planet over populated by human kind, estimates of the total number of species around us vary from ten million to eighty million.

One study estimates that in a single square meter of soil there may be nearly 1,000 different types of animals together forming a total population of 2 million individuals, many of these are invisible to human eyes. Yet scientists have so far been able to identify a total of some 1.5 million species of animals and 300,000 species of plants. (Foley, 1990)

Meanwhile, under the pretext of progress and development the world's heritage of biodiversity is being eroded at an alarming rate. 100 species are being lost on daily basis. Rainforest are being cleared, waterways are becoming wastelands, deserts are losing valuable genes that could help our crops adapt to new pressures.

1.3.6 Sustainable Development

The challenge of sustainable development is one of the most important issues facing society in the twenty-first century. Achieving economic growth and securing higher standard of living and quality of life should not be at the expense of the environment. Sustainable development is a pattern of resource use that aims to meet human needs while preserving the environment so that these needs can be met not only in the present but in the indefinite future.

The Brundtland Commission (1987) coined what has become the most often quoted definition of sustainable development as development that "meets the needs of the present without compromising the ability of future generations to meet their own needs". Protection and enhancement of the environment form one of the core principles of sustainable development. The field of sustainable development can conceptually be broken into three constituent parts:

    (a)   environmental sustainability,

    (b)   economic sustainability and

    (c)   Socio-political sustainability.

These three components are mutually reinforcing as observed by the United Nations (2005) World Summit Outcome Document that the three are interdependent and mutually reinforcing pillars of sustainable development although a fourth pillar, cultural diversity is being recognized as component of sustainable development.

Agenda 21, the earth summit work plan for environment and development issues in coming decades clearly identifies information, integration and participation as key building blocks to help countries achieve development and recognizes these interdependent pillars. It emphasizes that in sustainable development, everyone is a user and provider of information. If stressed the need to change from old sector-centered ways of doing business to new approaches that involve cross-sectoral co-ordination and the integration of environmental and social concerns into development processes. Agenda 21 further emphasized that broad public participation in decision making is a fundamental pre-requisite for achieving sustainable development.

The concept of sustainable development aligns with Botman concept on development without destruction i.e. every development must be ecologically and environmentally viable. Environmental sustainability is the process of making sure current processes of development interaction with the environment are pursued with the idea of keeping the environment as pristine as naturally possible, based on application of sound environmental management strategies. An unsustainable situation occurs when natural capital (the sum total of nature's resources) is used up faster than it can be replenished. Sustainability therefore requires that human activity only uses nature's resources at a rate at which they can be replenished.

1.3.7 Environmental Pollution

Pollution is an undesirable change in the physical, chemical or biological characteristics of the air, water or land that can be harmful to health, survival of human and other living organisms. Pollution is of Latin origin. It is a concept that is etymologically derived from the word "pollure" meaning to defile, to desecrate, to make unwholesome or to render unclean. There is several other dictionary definition of the pollution and they include: To destroy the purity or outrage the sanctity (Oxford), to make fowl, desecrate, to corrupt (Collins), to be fowl, to contaminate, to make offensive to human or plant life (Chambers).

In general, pollution could be defined as the direct or indirect introduction by man of substances or energy into the environment, capable of resulting in such deleterious effect such as harm to living resources, hazard to human health and living organisms, impairments of the quality use of the environment, aquatic, soil, air, aesthetic etc. Pollution can also be defined as the introduction of contaminants into the natural environment that causes adverse change. Pollution can take the form of chemical substances or energy, such as noise, heat or light. Pollutants, the components of pollution, can be either foreign substances/energies or naturally occurring contaminants. Pollution is often classed as point source or nonpoint source pollution. Water pollution that results in biological, chemical and physical alteration of the aquatic ecosystem creates a potential health hazard to human population that depends on the use of the aquatic resources as food and raw materials.

Similarly, soil pollution results from the introduction of contaminant into the soil, which presents a serious risk to the plant, animal and human health. Through the process of oxidation and corrosion, heavy metals become soluble and are leached into the soil from where they are picked up by growing plant thereby entering the food chain. It also leads to contamination of ground water while most of the metals and other contaminants get washed into streams and rivers during rain thereby contaminating the marine environment from where fishes and other aquatic organisms accumulate them in their tissue making them pose health risks to the consumers.

Gaseous emissions and particulate matters impair atmospheric air quality creating significant health risk to human population. Through developmental actions, various contaminants are being released inadvertently or intentionally by man to the environment. Broadly speaking sources of environmental pollution could be classified into:

- Domestic
- Industrial

- Oil and gas

- Transportation

- Power

- Agriculture

1.3.8 Environmental Inventory

This refers to taking inventory of the variables that represent the characteristics of the environment as it exists in an area where a particular project or activity is being considered. Compilation of the inventory is done from a checklist of descriptors common for the physical, biological, chemical, social, economic and cultural aspects of the environment. For instance, descriptors for the physical aspects of the environment include such major areas as geology, topography, climate, surface and ground water resources, water quality and air quality.

A common checklist helps to avoid over-looking any important inventory factor that could be affected by the proposed action. The use of checklist is particularly useful during screening stage which is one of the preliminary steps in environmental impact assessment process. It serves as the basis for evaluating the potential adverse and beneficial impacts of the proposed action.

1.3.9 Mitigation

Mitigation is developing all possible measures to ameliorate or reduce or even avoid the associated and potential impacts of the proposed action or project. The CEQ Regulation defines mitigation to include:

a. Avoiding the impact.

b. Minimizing the impact by limiting the degree or magnitude of the action.

c. Rectifying the impact by repairing, rehabilitating or restoring the affected environment.

d. Reducing or eliminating the impact overtime.

e. Compensating for the impacts by replacing or providing substitute resources or environment.

The study and commitment to mitigation measures have become an extensive and meaningful part of the EIA process. Potentially, adverse impacts can be avoided or mitigated to acceptable levels through careful design and implementation of appropriate measures or techniques to reduce the severity of the effects.

1.3.10 Environmental Management Plan (EMP)

Environmental Management Plan (EMP) is a critical component of an impact assessment process. It is an important tool that can be used to continuously measure and check the efficiency of the mitigation measures recommended by the impact assessment and incorporated into the project implementation process to minimize or eliminate identified negative impacts and enhance the beneficial impacts. EMP scope covers the environmental monitoring which is the systematic observation and measurement of variable in time and space. The effectiveness of an EIA is a function of the commitment to the implementation of the EMP. Having an EIA without EMP implementation is like having a car without an engine. This important component is discussed in details in chapter seven of this book.

1.3.11 Environmental Monitoring

Environmental monitoring as defined by UNEP (1996) is the systematic collection of environmental data through a series of repetitive measurement i.e. the systematic observation and measurement of environmental variables in time and space. Before the actual impact of a project on the environment can be determined, there is need to monitor selected variables.

Monitoring and measurement as specified in ISO 14001 Environmental Management System (EMS) requirement, which provides that organization shall establish, implement and maintain a procedure(s) to monitor and measure, on a regular basis, the key characteristics of its operations that can have a significant environmental impact. The procedures shall include the documenting of information to monitor performance, applicable operational controls and conformity with the organization's environmental objectives and targets.

To establish the actual impact of an action or project on human health and the ecological processes, environmental variables are measured over a period of time, such monitoring would require a monitoring program which is likely to be long lasting and require resources to be devoted in terms of technical manpower and funding. The degree and nature of resources required is a function of the nature of the project and predicted impact.

The FEPA EIA Procedure (1995) recognizes impact monitoring as the activity undertaken to identify variation in environmental parameters which can be attributed with confidence to the presence of a project or other course of action. Its role is to identify project-induced change and it can assist in the management of environmental effects by observing the extent of change and the degree of mitigation which is necessary. NEPA (1996) described three known types of environmental monitoring within the conceptual framework of environmental impact assessment as follows:

    i. Baseline Monitoring: This refers to the measurement of environmental parameters in the pre-project period.

    ii. Effects Monitoring: This involves the measurements of environmental parameters in the pre-project construction and implementation phases so as to detect changes in these parameters which can be attributed to the project.

    iii. Compliance Monitoring: This is the periodic or continuous measurement of environmental parameters or discharges to ensure that regulatory requirements and standards are met. Compliance monitoring can further be broken down into two i.e.

    iv. Mitigative measures monitoring which relates to the prescribed mitigation measures in the EIA reports.

    v. Regulatory compliance monitoring which relates to existing regulatory monitoring requirements.

Monitoring programmes provide the necessary and essential input in environmental auditing and can serve as a potent platform for providing early warning signal.

1.3.12 Environmental Auditing

Environmental Auditing is the organization and analysis of environmental monitoring data in order to establish the record of change associated with a project and the comparison of actual and predicted impact in order to determine the effectiveness of the impact assessment and management practices and procedures (FEPA, 1995). Environmental auditing rather than being fault finding is in the contrast fact-finding. Its benefits among others include:

    i. It helps in identifying accurate and inaccurate prediction.

    ii. It gives useful information in designing practical measures to mitigate actual impacts that have been observed.

    iii. Highlights positive efforts made in environmental performance.

    iv. Provides information on the level of commitment to mitigation measures proffered and helps in measuring the effectiveness of such measures.

v. It ensures compliance with environmental regulations.

vi. Enhances corporate image of the organization.

vii. Enhances the quality and effectiveness of the EIS.
Various types of environmental audits have been

identified to include:
1) Compliance Audit
2) Environmental Management System Audit
3) Risk Audit
4) Environmental Impairment Liability Audit
5) Environmental Marketing Audit
6) Energy Audit
7) Certification Audit
8) Due Diligence Audit
9) Environmental Performance Audit
10) Product Audit

The FEPA (1999) National Guidelines for Environmental Audit in

Nigeria identified six (6) environmental audit types:
I. Regulatory Compliance Audit (RCA);

II. Process Safety Audit;

III. Occupational Health Audit;

IV.   Product Quality Audit;

V.   Liability Audit; and

VI.   Management Audit

1.3.13 Administrative and Regulatory Framework

This includes the applicable environmental laws, regulations, policies, standards and requirements in which the EIA is carried out.

The regulatory framework provides the legal obligations which a given body, entity or government agency must subscribe in the quest to protect the environment through the use of relevant environment management tools such as the EIA. Existing statutes on environmental protection in Nigeria contains specific provisions designed to prohibit or control environmental pollution/degradation and also to prescribe sanctions or damages to be enforced against persons or corporate entities who contravene the provisions.

In Nigeria, the principal governmental bodies responsible for environmental matters and saddled with enforcing existing statutes and regulations are the Federal Ministry of Environment (FMEnv.) National Environmental Standards Regulatory and Enforcement Agency (NESREA) and the Department of Petroleum

Resources (DPR). The processes and application of EIA are governed principally by The Environmental Impact Assessment Decree 86 of 1992 and The Environmental Guidelines and Standards for the Petroleum Industry in Nigeria (EGASPIN) 1991.

These are however, derivable for a number of substantial national environmental laws that are pursuant to performing the constitutional responsibility of the Federal Government of Nigeria, which include protecting the environment. The Federal Republic of Nigeria Constitution (1999) stipulates that the state shall protect and improve the environment and safeguard the water, air and land, forest and wildlife. The applicable environmental laws that support EIA in Nigeria can be categorized under the following:

      I.   International
      ii. National
      iii. State
      iv. Local

The lists of some applicable International laws/legislations include:

Table 1.1: List of some applicable International Environmental Legislation

S/No.	Regulation	Year Adopted
1.	World Bank Environmental Assessment Source Books.	1998
2.	UN Convention on Biological Diversity.	1994
3.	UN Framework Convention on Climate Change.	1992
4.	International Convention on Oil Pollution Preparedness, Response and Cooperation.	1990
5.	Convention on the Control of Trans-boundary Movements of Hazardous Wastes and their Disposal of 1989 (Basel Convention).	1989
6.	Protocol on Substances that Deplete the Ozone Layer. *Note: The protocol was amended for the first time on 29 June 1990 in London. A second set of amendments was adopted in Copenhagen in November 1992; these entered into force on 1994.*	1987
7.	Convention for the Protection of the Ozone Layer.	1985
8.	UN Convention on the Law of the Sea.	1982
9.	Convention for Co-operation in the Protection and Development of the Marine and Coastal Environment of the West and Central African Region (Abidjan Convention).	1981
10.	Protocol Concerning Cooperation in Combating Pollution in Cases of Emergency in the West and Central African Region.	1981
11.	International Convention for the Prevention of Pollution from Ships (MARPOL 73/78).	1978
12.	International Convention on Standards of Training Certification and Watch-keeping for Seafarer (STCW).	1978
13.	Protocol Relating to the International Convention for the Safety of Life at Sea (SOLAS PROT).	1978
14.	International Convention for the Safety of Life at Sea (SOLAS).	1974
15.	Convention on the International Regulations for Preventing Collisions at Sea (COLREG).	1972
16.	Convention Concerning the Protection of the World Cultural and National Heritage (World Heritage Convention).	1972
17.	Convention on the Prevention of Marine Pollution By Dumping of Wastes and Other Matter. *Note: The Convention was amended in 1992*	1972
18.	International Convention on the Establishment of an International Fund for Compensation for Oil Pollution Damage (IOPC FUND).	1971
19.	International Convention on Civil Liability for Oil Pollution Damage (CLC).	1969
20.	African Convention on the Conservation of Nature and Natural Resources.	1968
21.	Convention on Facilitation of International Maritime Traffic.	1965
22.	Convention of the High Seas.	1958
23.	Convention on the Territorial Sea and Contiguous Zone.	1958
24.	Convention on the Continental Shelf (CSC).	1958
25.	International Convention for the Prevention of Pollution of the Sea by Oil (OILPOL).	1954

The list of some applicable Nigerian Environmental laws/regulations is as shown below

Table 1.2 : Nigerian Environmental Legislation

	Applicable Regulations	Year Adopted
1.	Environmental Impact Assessment Act (86)	1992
2.	Department of Petroleum Resources (DPR) Environmental Guidelines and	2002
3.	Procedure Guide for the Design and Construction of Oil and Gas Surface Production Facilities (DPR).	2001
4.	Mineral Oils (Safety) Regulations (DPR *Revised 1997*).	1997
5.	National Inland Waterways Authority Decree No. 13	1997
6.	Petroleum (Amendment) Regulations	1996
7.	Sectoral Guidelines for Oil and Gas Industry	1995
8.	Oil and Gas Pipelines Act and Regulations	1995
9.	Guidelines and Standards for Environmental Pollution Control in Nigeria • National Guidelines & Standards for Water Quality • National Guidelines & Standards for Waste Disposal through Underground Injection • National Guidelines on Environmentally Friendly Products & Eco-	1991/92
10.	National Environmental Protection Effluent Limitation Regulations – SI-8	1991/92
11.	Delta State Ministry of Environment and Natural Resources Edict	2003
12.	National Environmental Protection Pollution Abatement in Industries and Facilities Generating Wastes Regulations – SI-9	1991/92
13.	National Environmental Protection Management of Solid & Hazardous Wastes Regulations – SI-15	1991/92
14.	Harmful Wastes (Special Criminal Provisions, etc.) Act	1988
15.	Endangered Species (Control of International Trade and Traffic Act, 1985, CAP 108, LFN 1985)	1985
16.	Petroleum Pollution and Distribution (Anti-Sabotage) Act	1975
17.	Petroleum Act.	1969
18.	Oil in Navigable Waters Act.	1968
19.	Oil Pipelines Act	1956
20.	The Forestry Law of 1956	1963

1.3.14 Litigation

The law court influences the environmental assessment process through legal interpretation and enforcement. The law court interprets the provisions of the environmental laws, regulations and standards with respect to EIA processes and applications to enforce compliance. Non compliance and violation of provisions of the law by individuals or corporate bodies may attract sanctions, fines imprisonment and withdrawals of operating licenses of companies to enforce compliance.

1.4   Environmental Disasters

This section intends to discuss major environmental pollution issues on global scale that resulted in significant damages to the environment, public health and socio-economic life of the people within the zone of influence of its impacts. This is expected to build the consciousness and create sound awareness on the colossal damages of the adverse impacts from human development activities that occur, knowing that these impacts do have multidimensional consequences on environment, biodiversity, public health, reputation, and cost of remediation as well as litigation actions. This section is also to prepare the reader for better appreciation of the value of EIA as an important environmental management tool. These environmental disasters will be discussed using the following incidents

   a) Minimata disease in Japan
   b) Itai-Itai disease in Japan
   c) Love canal toxic waste incident

d) Bhopal gas leak disaster
e) Exxon Valdex oil spill incident
f) Deepwater horizon oil spill incident

1.4.1 Minimata Disease

Minamata disease is a neurological syndrome caused by severe mercury poisoning. The disease was first discovered in Minamata city in Kumamoto prefecture, Japan, in 1956. It was caused by the release of methyl mercury in the industrial waste water from the Chisso Corporation's chemical factory, which continued from 1932 to 1968. This highly toxic chemical bio accumulated in shellfish and fish in Minamata Bay and the Shiranui Sea, which, when eaten by the local populace, resulted in mercury poisoning. In the 1950s and early 1960s, hundreds of children around Japan's Minamata Bay were born with horrific birth defects after their mothers ate seafood contaminated with mercury compounds, which had been discharged into the bay since the 1930s while cat, dog, pig, and human deaths continued for 36 years (http://en.wikipedia.org/wiki/Minamata_disease)

Symptoms include ataxia, numbness in the hands and feet, general muscle weakness, narrowing of the field of vision, and damage to hearing and speech. In extreme cases, insanity, paralysis, coma, and death follow within weeks of the onset of symptoms.

As of March 2001, 2,265 victims had been officially recognized (1,784 of whom had died and over 10,000 had received financial compensation from Chisso. By 2004, Chisso Corporation had paid $86 million in compensation, and in the same year was ordered to clean up its contamination and a settlement was reached to compensate as-yet uncertified victims in 2010 **(National Institute for Minamata Disease (2001)**

1.4.2 Itai-Itai Disease

Itai-itai disease was the name given to the mass cadmium poisoning in Toyama Prefecture, Japan, between 1912 – 1932 following the consumption of seafood and rice contaminated with cadmium. The cadmium poisoning caused softening of the bones and kidney failure. The disease is named for the severe pains caused in the joints and spine. The term "itai-itai disease" was coined by locals which means it hurts me. The cadmium was released into rivers by mining companies in the mountains. The mining companies were successfully sued for the damage. Itai-itai disease is known as one of the Four Big Pollution Diseases of Japan.

Cadmium was released by mining operation controlled by the Mitsui Mining and Smelting Co., Ltd., which resulted in the pollution of the Jinzū River and its tributaries. The river was used not only for irrigation of rice fields, but also for drinking water, washing, fishing, and other uses by downstream populations. Due to the cadmium poisoning, the fish in the river started to die, and the rice irrigated with river water did not grow well. The cadmium and other heavy metals accumulated at the bottom of the river and in the water of the river. This water was then used to irrigate the rice fields. The rice absorbed heavy metals, especially the cadmium. The cadmium accumulated in the people eating contaminated rice.

The population complained to the Mitsui Mining and Smelting Company about the pollution. The company built a basin to store the mining waste water before leading it into the river. It was too little, too late as many people were already sick. The causes of the poisoning were not well understood and up to 1946, it was thought to be simply a regional disease or a type of bacterial infection.

Medical tests started in the 1940s and 1950s, searching for the cause of the disease. Initially, it was expected to be lead poisoning due to the lead mining upstream. Only in 1955 did Dr. Hagino and his colleagues suspected cadmium as the cause of the disease. Through investigation in 1961, it was determined that the Mitsui Mining and Smelting's Kamioka Mining Station caused the cadmium pollution and that the worst affected areas were 30

Prefecture began in 1971, and by 1977, 1500 hectares along the Jinzū River were designated for soil restoration. These farmers were compensated for lost crops as well as for lost production in past years by the Mitsui Mining and Smelting

In 1992, the average annual health expense compensation was ¥743 million. Agricultural damage was compensated with ¥1.75 billion per year, or a total of annually ¥2.518 billion. Another ¥620 million were invested annually to reduce further pollution of the river. On 17 March 2012, officials concluded the clean-up project of the cadmium-polluted areas in the Jinzū River basin. Eight-hundred sixty-three hectares of topsoil had been replaced since the clean-up began in 1979 at a total cost of ¥40.7 billion **(http://en.wikipedia.org/wiki/Itai-itai_disease).**

The project was financed by the Japanese national government, Mitsui Mining, and the Gifu and Toyama prefectural governments.

1.4.3 Love Canal Toxic Waste Incident
Love Canal, a neighborhood in Niagara Falls, New York became the subject of national and international attention in the mid-1970s after it was revealed in the press that the site had formerly been used to bury 21,000 tons of toxic waste by Hooker Chemical Company (now Occidental Petroleum Corporation).

Hooker Chemical sold the site to the Niagara Falls School Board in 1953 with a deed explicitly detailing the presence of the waste and including a liability limitation clause about the contamination. The construction efforts of housing development, combined with particularly heavy rainstorms, released the chemical waste, leading to a public health emergency and an urban planning scandal. Hooker Chemical was found to be negligent in their disposal of waste, though not reckless in the sale of the land, in what became a test case for liability clauses. The dumpsite was discovered and investigated by the local newspaper, the Niagara Falls Gazette, from 1976 through 1978.

Ten years after the incident, New York State Health Department stated that Love Canal would long be remembered as a "national symbol of a failure to exercise a sense of concern for future generations."The Love Canal incident was especially significant as a situation where the inhabitants "overflowed into the wastes instead of the other way around."

The canal used by local children to swim in the summer and skated in the winter in the 1920s became a dump site for the City of Niagara Falls, with the city regularly unloading its municipal refuse into the pit until in 1948 after World War II when Hooker became sole user and owner of the site until 1953. During this time, 21,000 tons of chemicals such as "caustics, alkalines, fatty acids and chlorinated hydrocarbons from the manufacturing of dyes, perfumes, solvents for rubber and synthetic resins" were added. These chemicals were buried at a depth of twenty to twenty-five feet. After 1953, the canal was covered with soil, and vegetation began to grow atop the dumpsite **(http://en.wikipedia.org/wiki/Love_Canal)**.

In 1976, two reporters for the Niagara Falls Gazette, David Pollak and David Russell, tested several sump pumps near Love Canal and found toxic chemicals in them. The matter went quiet for more than a year and was resurrected by reporter Michael Brown, who then investigated potential health effects by carrying forth an informal door-to-door survey in early 1978, finding birth defects and many anomalies such as enlarged feet, heads, hands, and legs. He advised the local residents to create a protest group, which was led by resident Karen Schroeder, whose daughter had many (about a dozen) birth defects. The New York State Health Department followed suit and found an abnormal incidence of miscarriages. The dumpsite was declared an unprecedented state emergency on August 2, 1978.

According to the United States Environmental Protection Agency (EPA) in 1979, residents exhibited a "disturbingly high rate of miscarriages ... Love Canal can now be added to a growing list of environmental disasters involving toxics, ranging from industrial workers stricken by nervous disorders and cancers to the discovery of toxic materials in the milk of nursing mothers." In one case, two out of four children in a single Love Canal family had birth defects; one girl was born deaf with a cleft palate, an extra row of teeth, and slight retardation, and a boy was born with an eye defect (http://www.epa.gov/history/topics/lovecanal)

A survey conducted by the Love Canal Homeowners Association found that 56% of the children born from 1974–1978 had at least one birth defect By 1978, Love Canal had become a national media event with articles referring to the neighborhood as "a public health time bomb," and "one of the most appalling environmental tragedies in American history." On August 7, 1978, United States President Jimmy Carter announced a federal health emergency, called for the allocation of federal funds and ordered the Federal Disaster Assistance Agency to assist the City of Niagara Falls to remedy the Love Canal site.

This was the first time in American history that emergency funds were used for a situation other than a natural disaster. Carter had trenches built that would transport the wastes to sewers and had home sump pumps sealed off. Through scientific studies eleven known or suspected carcinogens was identified, one of the most prevalent being benzene. There was also dioxin (polychlorinated dibenzodioxins) in the water, a very hazardous substance (http://en.wikipedia. org/wiki/Love_Canal).

In 1979, EPA announced the result of blood tests that showed high white blood cell counts, a precursor to leukemia and chromosome damage in Love Canal residents, and that 33% of the residents had undergone chromosomal damage. The United States National Research Council (NRC) surveyed Love Canal health studies in 1991 and noted that the major exposure of concern was the groundwater which led to exposure through air and soil. The study also noted that exposed children were found to have an "excess of seizures, learning problems, hyperactivity, eye irritation, skin rashes, abdominal pain, and incontinence" and stunted growth. (National Research Council, Committee on Environmental Epidemiology, 1991)

Eventually, the government relocated more than 800 families and reimbursed them for their homes, and the United States Congress passed the Comprehensive Environmental Response, Compensation, and Liability Act (CERCLA), or the Superfund Act. It is called "Superfund" because of the fund established by the act to help the clean-up of toxic pollution in residential locations such as Love Canal. It has been stated that Love Canal has "become the symbol for what happens when hazardous industrial products are not confined to the workplace but 'hit people where they live' in inestimable amounts (http://en.wikipedia.org /wiki/Love_Canal).

In 1979, EPA announced the result of blood tests that showed high white blood cell counts, a precursor to leukemia and chromosome damage in Love Canal residents, and that 33% of the residents had undergone chromosomal damage. The United States National Research Council (NRC) surveyed Love Canal health studies in 1991 and noted that the major exposure of concern was the groundwater which led to exposure through air and soil. The study also noted that exposed children were found to have an "excess of seizures, learning problems, hyperactivity, eye irritation, skin rashes, abdominal pain, and incontinence" and stunted growth. (National Research Council, Committee on Environmental Epidemiology, 1991)

Eventually, the government relocated more than 800 families and reimbursed them for their homes, and the United States Congress passed the Comprehensive Environmental Response, Compensation, and Liability Act (CERCLA), or the Superfund Act. It is called "Superfund" because of the fund established by the act to help the clean-up of toxic pollution in residential locations such as Love Canal. It has been stated that Love Canal has "become the symbol for what happens when hazardous industrial products are not confined to the workplace but 'hit people where they live' in inestimable amounts (http://en.wikipedia.org /wiki/Love_Canal).

1.4.4 Bhopal gas leak tragedy

The Bhopal disaster, also referred to as the Bhopal gas tragedy, was a gas leak incident in India, considered the world's worst industrial disaster. It occurred on the nights of December 2- 3, 1984 at the Union Carbide India Limited (UCIL) pesticide plant in Bhopal. Over 500,000 people were exposed to methyl isocyanate (MIC) gas and other chemicals. The toxic substance made its way in and around the shanty towns located near the plant. Estimates vary on the death toll. The official immediate death toll was 2,259.

The government of Madhya Pradesh confirmed a total of 3,787 deaths related to the gas release (http://en.wikipedia.org/wiki/Bhopal disaster). Others estimated 8,000 deaths within two weeks and another 8,000 or more have since died from gas-related diseases. A government affidavit in 2006 stated the leak caused 558,125 injuries including 38,478 temporary partial injuries and approximately 3,900 severely and permanently disabling injuries (http://www.webcitation.org)

The cause of the disaster remains under debate. However, it was established that about 30 metric tons of methyl isocyanate (MIC) escaped from the MIC holding tank as a result of exothermic reaction, releasing a large volume of toxic gases to the atmosphere in 45 to 60 minutes. The gases were blown in southeastern direction over Bhopal. Apart from MIC, the gas cloud may have contained phosgene, hydrogen cyanide, carbon monoxide, hydrogen chloride, oxides of nitrogen, monomethyl amine (MMA) and carbon dioxide, either produced in the storage tank or in the atmosphere. The gas cloud composition was composed mainly of materials denser than the surrounding air, stayed close to the ground and spread outwards through the surrounding community.

The initial effects of exposure were coughing, severe eye irritation and a feeling of suffocation, burning in the respiratory tract, blepharospasm, breathlessness, and stomach pains as well as vomiting. People awakened by these symptoms fled away from the plant. Those who ran inhaled more than those who had a vehicle to ride. Owing to their height, children and other people of shorter stature inhaled higher concentrations. Thousands of people had died by the following morning. Primary causes of deaths were choking, reflexogenic circulatory collapse and pulmonary oedema.

Findings during autopsies revealed changes not only in the lungs but also cerebral oedema, tubular necrosis of the kidneys, fatty degeneration of the liver and necrotisingenteritis. The stillbirth rate increased by up to 300% and neo-natal mortality rate by around 200% as trees in the vicinity became barren within a few days and 2,000 bloated animal carcasses had to be disposed of. 170,000 people were treated at hospitals and temporary dispensaries. 2,000 buffalo, goats, and other animals were collected and buried.

Supplies, including food, became scarce owing to suppliers' safety fears. Fishing was prohibited in the Narmada River where bodies were dumped causing further supply shortages. (http://en.wikipedia.org/wiki/Bhopal_disaster) A number of clinical studies performed revealed the following long term health effects among others.
- Eyes: Chronic conjunctivitis, scars on cornea, corneal opacities,   early cataracts
- Respiratory tracts: Obstructive and/or restrictive disease, pulmonary fibrosis, aggravation of TB and chronic bronchitis
- Neurological system: Impairment of memory, finer motor skills, numbness etc.
- Psychological problems: Post traumatic stress disorder (PTSD)
- Children's health: Peri- and neonatal death rates increased. Failure to grow, intellectual impairment etc (Eckerman Ingrid, 2005).

Other health effect still being studied include: female reproduction, chromosomal aberrations, cancer, immune deficiency, neurological post traumatic stress disorder (PTSD).

In 1989, UCC paid $470m ($907m in 2014 dollars) to settle litigation stemming from the disaster. In 1994, UCC sold its stake in UCIL to Eveready Industries India Limited (EIIL), which subsequently merged with McLeod Russel (India) Ltd. Eveready Industries India Limited ended clean-up on the site in 1998, when it terminated its 99-year lease and turned over control of the site to the state government of Madhya Pradesh. Dow Chemical Company purchased UCC in 2001, seventeen years after the disaster.

Civil and criminal cases are pending in the District Court of Bhopal, India, involving UCC and Warren Anderson, UCC CEO at the time of the disaster. In June 2010, seven ex-employees, including the former UCIL chairman, were convicted in Bhopal of causing death by negligence and sentenced to two years imprisonment and a fine of about $2,000 each, the maximum punishment allowed by Indian law. An eighth former employee was also convicted, but died before the judgment was passed on Bhopal gas leak tragedy. By the end of October 2003, according to the Bhopal Gas Tragedy Relief and Rehabilitation Department, compensation had been awarded to 554,895 people for injuries received and 15,310 survivors of those killed. The average amount to families of the dead was $2,200 (Broughton Edward, 2005)

1.4.5 Exxon Valdez Oil Spill

The Exxon Valdez oil spill occurred in Prince William Sound, Alaska, on March 24, 1989, when Exxon Valdez, an oil tanker bound for Long Beach, California, struck Prince William Sound's Bligh Reef and spilled 260,000 to 750,000 barrels of crude oil over the next few days (http://en.wikipedia.org/wiki/Exxon_Valdez_oil_spill).

It was considered to be one of the most devastating human-caused environmental disasters with both the long-term and short-term effects of the oil spill having been studied. Immediate effects included the deaths of 100,000 to as many as 250,000 seabirds, at least 2,800 sea otters, 300 harbor seals, 247 Bald Eagles, and 22 Orcas, and an unknown number of salmon and herring. The Valdez spill was the largest ever in US waters until the 2010 Deepwater Horizon oil spill, in terms of volume released. The oil, originally extracted at the Prudhoe Bay oil field, eventually covered 1,300 miles (2,100 km) of coastline and 11,000 square miles (28,000 km2) of ocean (Brandon Keim, 2009).

The disaster resulted in International Maritime Organization introducing comprehensive marine pollution prevention rules (MARPOL) through various conventions. The rules were ratified by member countries and under International Ship Management rules, the ships are being operated with a common objective of "safer ships and cleaner oceans".

In addition to the spill incident, it was reported that the dispersant used for the clean-up was toxic. The main component of the dispersant used for the clean-up "Corexit9580", 2-butoxyethanol was identified as toxic and "one of the agents that caused liver, kidney, lung, nervous system, and blood disorders among clean-up crews in Alaska following the 1989 Exxon Valdez spill. According to media reports, nearly all of the individuals in those crews have died, with the average age of death around 50.

Oiled shoreline (Workers using high-pressure, hot-water washing to clean an oiled shoreline). (http://en.wikipedia.org/wiki/Exxon_Valdez_oil_spill

Exxon Valdez Coastline devastation and clean up (Brandon Keim, 2009)

Dead bird species from the incident
(http://en.wikipedia.org/wiki/Exxon_Valdez_oil_spill

Because Prince William Sound contained many rocky coves where the oil collected, the decision was made to displace it with high-pressure hot water. However, this also displaced and destroyed the microbial populations on the shoreline; many of these organisms (e.g. plankton) are the basis of the coastal marine food chain, and others (e.g. certain bacteria and fungi) are capable of facilitating the biodegradation of oil. At the time, both scientific advice and public pressure was to clean everything, but since then, a much greater understanding of natural and facilitated remediation processes has developed, due somewhat in part to the opportunity presented for study by the Exxon Valdez spill. Despite the extensive cleanup attempts, less than ten percent of the oil was recovered and a study conducted by NOAA determined that as of early 2007 more than 26 thousand U.S. gallons (98 m3) of oil remain in the sandy soil of the contaminated shoreline, declining at a rate of less than 4% per year (Jewett SC et al, 2001).

In 2003, fifteen years after the spill, a team from the University of North Carolina found that the remaining oil was lasting far longer than anticipated, which in turn had resulted in more long-term loss of many species than had been expected. The researchers found that at only a few parts per billion, polycyclic aromatic hydrocarbons caused a long-term increase in mortality rates. They reported that "species as diverse as sea otters, harlequin ducks and killer whales suffered large, long-term losses and that oiled mussel beds and other tidal shoreline habitats will take an estimated 30 years to recover (Williamson, David, 2003). According to several studies funded by the state of Alaska, the spill had both short-term and long-term economic effects. These included the loss of recreational sports, fisheries, reduced tourism and an estimate of what economists call "existence value", which is the value to the public of a pristine Prince William Sound. The economy of the city of Cordova, Alaska was adversely affected after the spill damaged stocks of salmon and herring in the area.

In 2006, a study done by the National Marine Fisheries Service in Juneau found that about 9.6 kilometres of shoreline around Prince William Sound was still affected by the spill, with 101.6 tonnes of oil remaining in the area. The effects of the spill continued to be felt for many years afterwards. As of 2010 there were an estimated 23,000 US gallons of Valdez crude oil are still in Alaska's sand and soil, breaking down at a rate estimated at less than 4% per year (http://www.abc.net.au/news/2006-05-17/exxon-valdez-oil-spill-still-a-threat-study) . Exxon spent an estimated $2 billion cleaning up the spill and a further $1 billion to settle related civil and criminal charges. In addition, Exxon paid the sum of $507.5 million as punitive damages after challenging the ruling for it to pay the sum $287 million for actual damages and $5 billion for punitive damages(http://en.wikipedia.org/wiki/Exxon_Valdez_oil_spill).

Though recent studies show significant species recovery at the impacted area, the ecological impact of the spill 25 years after is still being observed. On March 24, 2014, the twenty-fifth anniversary of the spill, NOAA scientists reported that some species seem to have recovered, with the sea otter the latest creature to return to pre-spill numbers. Scientists who have monitored the spill area for the last 25 years report that concern remains for one of two pods of local orca whales, with fears that one pod may eventually die out. Federal scientists estimate that between 16,000 and 21,000 gallons of oil remains on beaches in Prince William Sound and up to 450 miles away. Some of the oil does not appear to have biodegraded at all. A USGS scientist who analyses the remaining oil along the coastline states that it remains among rocks and between tide marks(http://www.pbs.org/newshour/updates/25-years-later-scientists-remember-exxon-valdez-spill)

1.4.6 The BP oil spill disaster

The Deepwater Horizon oil spill also referred to as the BP oil spill, the BP oil disaster, the Gulf of Mexico oil spill, and the Macondo blowout began on 20 April 2010 in the Gulf of Mexico on the BP-operated Macondo Prospect. It claimed eleven lives and is considered the largest accidental marine oil spill in the history of the petroleum industry, an estimated 8% to 31% larger in volume than the previously largest(Exxon Vadez) (Robertson and Krauss, 2010). Following the explosion and sinking of the Deepwater Horizon oil rig, a sea-floor oil gusher flowed for 87 days releasing an estimated 4.9 million barrels of crude oil to the sea until it was capped on 15th July, 2010). After several failed efforts to contain the flow, the well was declared sealed on 19th September 2010.

Following the spill a massive response ensued to protect beaches, wetlands and estuaries from the spreading oil utilizing skimmer ships, floating booms, controlled burns and 1.84 million US gallons of Corexit oil dispersant. Due to the 3 months-long spill, along with adverse effects from the response and cleanup activities, extensive damage to marine and wildlife habitats and fishing and tourism industries were reported. In Louisiana, 4.6 million pounds of oily material was removed from the beaches in 2013, over double the amount collected in (http://www.npr.org/for-bp-cleanup-2013) . Oil cleanup crews worked four days a week on 55 miles of Louisiana shoreline throughout 2013. Oil continued to be found as far from the

Macondo site as the waters off the Florida Panhandle and Tampa Bay, where scientists said the oil and dispersant mixture is embedded in the sand (http://www.tampabay.com/news/environment/water/oil-from-bp-spill)

In 2013 it was reported that dolphins and other marine life continued to die in record numbers with infant dolphins dying at six times the normal rate. (http://news.discovery.com). One study released in 2014 reported that tuna and amberjack that were exposed to oil from the spill developed deformities of the heart and other organs that would be expected to be fatal or at least life-shortening and another study found that cardiotoxicity might have been widespread in animal life exposed to the spill.

In November 2012, BP and the United States Department of Justice settled federal criminal charges with BP pleading guilty to 11 counts of manslaughter, two misdemeanors, and a felony count of lying to Congress. BP also agreed to four years of government monitoring of its safety practices and ethics and the Environmental Protection Agency announced that BP would be temporarily banned from new contracts with the US government. BP and the Department of Justice agreed to a record-setting $4.525 billion in fines and other payments but further legal proceedings not expected to conclude until 2014 are ongoing to determine payouts and fines under the Clean Water Act and the Natural Resources Damage Assessment. As of February 2013, criminal and civil settlements and payments to a trust fund had cost the company $42.2 billion (http://en.wikipedia.org/wiki/ Deepwater_Horizon_oil_spill)

According to the satellite images data, the spill directly impacted 68,000 square miles (180,000 km2) of ocean(SkyTruth, 2010) By early June 2010, oil had washed up on 125 miles (201 km) of Louisiana's coast and along the Mississippi, Florida, and Alabama coastlines. Oil sludge appeared in the Intracoastal Waterway and on Pensacola Beach and the Gulf Islands National Seashore. In late June, (which year), oil reached Gulf Park Estates, its first appearance in Mississippi. In July 2011, tar balls reached Grand Isle and the shores of Lake Pontchartrain. In September, a new wave of oil suddenly coated 16 miles (26 km) of Louisiana coastline and marshes west of the Mississippi River in Plaquemines Parish.

In October, weathered oil reached Texas and as of July 2011, about 491 miles (790 km) of coastline in Louisiana, Mississippi, Alabama and Florida were contaminated by oil and a total of 1,074 miles (1,728 km) had been oiled since the spill began. As of December 2012, 339 miles (546 km) of coastline remain subject to evaluation and/or cleanup operations.

Deepwater horizon explosion   Oil from the Horizon oil spill
approaches the coast of Alaska (http://en.wikipedia.org)

Oil stained beaches in Pensacola, Florida Thick oil washes
ashore in Louisiana; (http://en.wikipedia.org)

Concerns were raised about the appearance of underwater, horizontally-extended plumes of dissolved oil. Researchers concluded that deep plumes of dissolved oil and gas would likely remain confined to the northern Gulf of Mexico and that the peak impact on dissolved oxygen would be delayed and long lasting (Adcroft, A., R et al, 2010). As of January 2011, tar balls, oil sheen trails, fouled wetlands marsh grass and coastal sands were still evident. Subsurface oil remained offshore and in fine silts. In April 2012, oil was still found along as much as 200 miles (320 km) of Louisiana coastline and tar balls continued to wash up on the barrier islands. In 2013, some scientists at the Gulf of Mexico Oil Spill and Ecosystem Science Conference said that as much as one-third of the oil may have mixed with deep ocean sediments, where it risks damage to ecosystems and commercial fisheries

The spill area hosts 8,332 species, including more than 1,270 fish, 604 polychaetes, 218 birds, 1,456 mollusks, 1,503 crustaceans, 4 sea turtles and 29 marine mammals (Tunnell W et al., 2010). Between May and June 2010, the spill waters contained 40 times more Polycyclic aromatic hydrocarbons (PAH)'s than before the spill. PAHs are often linked to oil spills and include carcinogens and chemicals that pose various health risks to humans and marine life. The PAHs were most concentrated near the Louisiana Coast, but levels also jumped 2–3 folds in areas off Alabama, Mississippi and Florida. PAHs can harm marine species directly and microbes used to consume the oil can reduce marine oxygen levels.

The oil contained approximately 40% methane by weight, compared to about 5% found in typical oil deposits (http://www.reuters.com/ article/2010/us-oil-spill-carcinogens) . Methane can potentially suffocate marine life and create "dead zones" where oxygen is depleted.

A 2014 study of the effects of the oil spill on bluefin tuna funded by National Oceanic and Atmospheric Administration (NOAA), Stanford University, and the Monterey Bay Aquarium and published in the journal Science; found that the toxins from oil spills can cause irregular heartbeats leading to cardiac arrest. Calling the vicinity of the spill "one of the most productive ocean ecosystems in the world", the study found that even at very low concentrations "PAH cardiotoxicity was potentially a common form of injury among a broad range of species in the vicinity of the oil." (Sahagun, Louis, 2014).

Another peer-reviewed study, released in March 2014 and conducted by 17 scientists from the United States and Australia and published in the Proceedings of the National Academy of Sciences, found that tuna and amberjack that were exposed to oil from the spill developed deformities of the heart and other organs that would be expected to be fatal or at least life-shortening. The scientists said that their findings would most likely apply to other large predator fish and "even to humans, whose developing hearts are in many ways similar." (Wines, Michael, 2014)

An oiled Brown Pelican heavily-oiled young turtles 20 to 40 miles offshore captured for rehabilitation near Grande Isle, Louisiana (http://en.wikipedia.org/wiki/Deepwater_Horizon_oil_spill)

Striped dolphins (Stenellacoeruleoalba) observed in emulsified oil heavy oiling of Bay Jimmy, Plaquemines Parish (http://en.wikipedia.org/wiki/Deepwater_Horizon_oil_spill

By June 2010, 143 spill-exposure cases had been reported to the Louisiana Department of Health and Hospitals. 108 of those involved are workers in the clean-up efforts, while 35 were reported by residents. Chemicals from the oil and dispersant are believed to be the cause; it is believed that the addition of dispersants made the oil more toxic.

A 2012 survey of the health effects of the spill on cleanup workers reported "eye, nose and throat irritation; respiratory problems; blood in urine, vomit and rectal bleeding; seizures; nausea and violent vomiting episodes that last for hours; skin irritation, burning and lesions; short-term memory loss and confusion; liver and kidney damage; central nervous system effects and nervous system damage; hypertension and miscarriages". In addition the report warned that "chronic adverse health effects, including cancers, liver and kidney disease, mental health disorders, birth defects and developmental disorders should be anticipated among sensitive populations and those most heavily exposed"

(http://en.wikipedia.org/wiki/Deepwater_Horizon_oil_spill
The spill had a strong economic impact to BP as also the Gulf Coast's economy sectors such as offshore drilling, fishing and tourism. On BP's expenditures on the spill included the cost of the spill response, containment, relief well drilling, grants to the Gulf States, claims paid and federal costs, including fines and penalties.

As of March 2012, BP estimated the company's total spill-related expenses do not exceed $37.2 billion. However, by some estimation penalties that BP may be required to pay have reached as high as $90 billion. In addition, in November 2012 the EPA announced that BP will be temporarily banned from seeking new contracts with the US government. Due to the loss of the market value, BP dropped from the second to the fourth largest of the four major oil companies by 2013. During the crisis, BP gas stations in the United States reported sales-off between 10 and 40% due to backlash against the company (http://en.wikipedia.org/wiki/Deepwater_Horizon_oil_spill)

Chapter Two

PURPOSE, OBJECTIVES AND SCOPE OF EIA

This chapter discuses the purpose, scope and objectives of EIA, EIA mandatory activities, tools and resources required for EIA.

The environment as being expressed by media coverage has become a topical issue of significance to humanity. This is obviously due to the need to address the challenges posed by the deterioration of human environment. Foley (1991) observed that the deterioration of human environment is not just an obscure scientific theory or remote and implausible threat which has been blown out of proportion by irresponsible media coverage but it is a danger of practical importance facing human race. As the degree of degradation and deterioration of the environment is increasing, so also is the degree of devastation suffered by man.

According to the Nigerian National Guidelines on Pollution Prevention, industrialization is inevitable because it is vital to a nation's socio-economic development as it provides ready employment opportunities for a good percentage of the population in medium to highly developed economies. However, various devastating ecological and human disasters which have continuously occurred over the last three decades or so implicate industries as major contributors to environmental degradation and pollution problems of various magnitudes. Industries vary according to process technology, size and nature of products, characteristics and complexity of wastes discharged. Industrial wastes and emissions contain toxic and hazardous substances most of which can be detrimental to human health.

Human quest for development has continued to result in anthropogenic ecological disasters. The past 20 years have seen a growing realization that the current model of development is unsustainable. From the loss of biodiversity with the felling of rainforest or overfishing, to the negative impact of industrial activities and consumption patterns are having on the environment and climate (global warming and climate change). It is clear that our way of life is placing an increasing burden on the planet. The increasing stress, which man is exerting on resources and the environmental systems such as water, land and air seems to be on the increase, especially as the world's population continue to increase and we already see a world where over a billion people live on less than a dollar a day where more than 800 million malnourished and over 2.5 billion lack access to adequate sanitation and clean environment.

The global phenomenon depicts the picture of the Nigeria's experience. As documented in the vision 2010 report on ecology and the Nigerian environment. Nigeria has a total land area of 923,773 square kilometers and is richly endowed with abundant and diverse natural resources both renewable and non-renewable. The country is blessed with mineral, physical, biological and energy resources. From the mangrove and rainforest of the south through the various savannah and semi-arid ecosystems of the north, the nation is richly endowed with fisheries resources, wildlife, timber, medicinal plants, water, ornaments and food crops, animal including human resources.

However, these resources are being exploited in an uncoordinated and uncontrolled manner, a situation that has led to over exploitation of some, depletion of others and outright abuse of the utilization of some and even extinction of other species. In addition to these patterns of exploitation, the environment is constantly polluted and degraded by industrial activities and through project implementation. The carrying capacity of the environment is being threatened and there are visible and verifiable indicators of significant environmental impacts and ecological disasters across the length and breadth of the country. Today, the Nigerian environment is faced with many ecological and environmental problems as outlined below by the Vision 2010 Report. They include:
   a) Drought and desertification in the north.
   b) Severe gully erosions in the eastern and northern states.

c) Coastal and marine erosion in coastal and riverine states.

d) Flooding in low-lying belt of mangrove and freshwater swamps along the coast.

e) Uncontrolled logging with inherent problems of the destruction of biodiversity.

f) Inappropriate agricultural practices.

g) Destruction of watershed.

h) Soil-crust formation caused by loss of water.

i) Destruction of agricultural lands.

j) Creation of burrow pits associated with bad mining practices and road works.

k) Oil pollution from spillage and gas flaring related problems.

l) Industrial pollution, municipal waste generation and urban decay.

The list is not exhaustive, what is clear here is that there are wide ranging anthropogenic environmental effects of human interactions with the environment in the course of development.

Given that for life to continue unabated, there must be a balance between development and environment. The environment that is, the life support system must be maintained sustainably. As concern has grown worldwide about environmental degradation and the threat it poses to human well being and economic development, many industrial and developing nations, as well as donor agencies, have incorporated environmental assessment procedures into their decision making process, thereby promoting the philosophy of industrialization that strike a balance between socio-economic and environmental considerations

Since the evolution of EIA in 1969 in the USA and the promulgation of Decree 86 of 1992 in Nigeria, EIA has become a potent management tool that helps managers and policy makers make balanced decision with respect to environmental protection in the total public interest. The foregoing discussions were intended to provide the platform for clear understanding of the purpose of an EIA; this understanding will further be boosted by leveraging on the provisions of some relevant laws, policies and standards as shown below.

The World Bank Environmental Assessment Policy emphasizes identification of environmental issues early in project cycle, designing environmental improvement into projects and avoiding mitigation or compensating for adverse impacts; the intent is to ensure that development options under consideration are environmentally sound and sustainable. This explains why the World Bank makes environmental assessment a fundamental condition and administration on projects and development options. The EIA Act No 86 of 1992 makes EIA mandatory for all new major public and private projects in Nigeria. This is necessary to consider the likely impacts and the extent of these impacts on the environment before embarking on any project or activity. The National Policy on Environment (1989) describes the guidelines and strategies for achieving the policy goal of sustainable development by:

   a) Securing for all Nigerians a quality of environment adequate for their health and well being.

   b) Conserving and using the natural resources for the benefit of present and future generation.

   c) Restoring, maintaining and enhancing the ecosystem as well as ecological processes that are essential for the preservation of biological diversity.

   d) Raising public awareness and promoting understanding of the essential linkages between the environment, resources and development.

   e) Collaboration with other countries, international organizations and agencies to achieve optimal use of trans-boundary cooperation in order to protect environmental resources.

The International Finance Corporation (IFC) applies the Performance Standards to manage social and environmental risks and impacts and to enhance development opportunities in private sector financing in its member countries eligible for financing. There are eight performance standards established that the client is to meet throughout the life of an investment by IFC or other relevant financial institution. They include:

Performance Standard1: Social and Environmental Assessment and Management System

Performance Standard 2: Labour and Working Conditions

Performance Standard 3: Pollution Prevention and Abatement

Performance Standard 4: Community Health, Safety and Security

Performance Standard5: Land Acquisition and Involuntary Resettlement

Performance Standard6: Biodiversity Conservation and Sustainable Natural Resources Management

Performance Standard 7: Indigenous People

Performance Standard 8: Cultural Heritage

Performance Standard 1 establishes the importance of the following:

(i) Integrated assessment to identify social and environmental impacts, risks, and opportunities of project.

(ii) Effective community engagement through disclosure of project related information and consultation with local communities on matters that directly affect them

(iii) The client's management of social and environmental performance throughout the life of the project.

The IFC Performance Standard1underscores the importance of managing social and environmental performance throughout the life of a project (any business activity that is subject to assessment and management). Drawing on the elements of the established business management process of "Plan, Implement, Check and Act", the system entails the thorough assessment of potential social and environmental impacts and risks from the early stages of project development and provides order and consistency for mitigating and managing these on an ongoing basis. It recognizes that a good management system appropriate to the size and nature of a project promotes sound and sustainable social and environmental performance and can lead to improved financial, social and environmental project outcomes. The scope of the application of the performance standard applies to projects with social or environmental risks and impacts that should be managed in the early stages of project development and on an ongoing basis.

Performance Standards 2 through to 8 establish the requirements to avoid, reduce, mitigate or compensate for impacts on people and the environment and to improve work conditions where appropriate. While all relevant social and environmental risks and potential impacts should be considered as part of assessment, Performance Standard 2 through 8 describes potential social and environmental impacts that require particular attention in emerging markets. The client is required to manage its social and environmental impacts through its Social and Environmental

Management System consistent with Performance Standard 1 requirements.

Similarly, The Equator Principles (EPs) which is a risk management framework, adopted by financial institutions for determining, assessing and managing environmental and social risk in projects apply globally to all industry sectors and to four financial products 1) Project Finance Advisory Services 2) Project Finance 3) Project-Related Corporate Loans and 4) Bridge Loans. The relevant thresholds and criteria for application is described in detail in the Scope section of the EP and is primarily intended to provide a minimum standard for due diligence to support responsible risk decision-making. Currently 80 Equator Principles Financial Institutions (EPFIs) in 34 countries have officially adopted the EPs, covering over 70 percent of international Project Finance debt in emerging markets.

EPFIs commit to implementing the EP in their internal environmental and social policies, procedures and standards for financing projects and will not provide Project Finance or Project-Related Corporate Loans to projects where the client will not, or is unable to, comply with the EP. While the EP are not intended to be applied retroactively, EPFIs apply them to the expansion or upgrade of an existing project where changes in scale or scope may create significant environmental and social risks and impacts, or significantly change the nature or degree of an existing impact.

The EPs have greatly increased the attention and focus on social/community standards and responsibility, including robust standards for indigenous peoples, labour standards, and consultation with locally affected communities within the Project Finance market. They have also promoted convergence around common environmental and social standards. Multilateral development banks, including the European Bank for Reconstruction & Development and export credit agencies through the OECD Common Approaches are increasingly drawing on the same standards as the EPs. The EPs have also helped spur the development of other responsible environmental and social management practices in the financial sector and banking industry (for example, Carbon Principles in the US, Climate Principles worldwide) and have provided a platform for engagement with a broad range of interested stakeholders, including non-governmental organisations (NGOs), clients and industry bodies.

The purpose of EIA therefore as captioned by the World Bank EA Source Book is to ensure that the development options under consideration are environmentally sound and sustainable and that any environmental consequences are recognized early in the project cycle and taken into account in the project design and implementation. The overall purpose of EIA is to improve the sustainability of the project within its proposed environment and lead to be more efficient use of resources.

2.1 Objectives of EIA

a) To establish the baseline condition of the physical, chemical, biological and socio-cultural and health environment around the proposed site and within the area of influence prior to project implementation.

b) To identify, predict and assess the associated as well as potential impacts of the proposed project/action on the receiving environment.

c) To identify ways of improving project's environmental sustainability and mitigating adverse impacts.

d) To enable project planners address environmental issues in a timely and practical fashion.

e) To obtain regulatory approvals for project execution.

f) To build public confidence in the planning process by providing for public participation and consultation.

g) To promote improved social-land environmental performance of organizations and companies.

2.2 Types of EIA

The World Bank Operational Directive (OD) on Environmental Assessment recognizes three types of EIA:

1) Project Specific EIA: Are used to analyze specific investment projects (e.g. dams, factories, irrigations, oil and gas developments etc.) with significant environmental issues. A project-specific EIA normally cover existing environmental baseline conditions, potential environmental impacts, systematic environmental comparison of

alternatives projects, sites, technologies and designs, mitigation measures, environmental management plan, training and monitoring.

2) Regional EIA: Are used where a number of significant development activities with potentially cumulative impacts are planned for a reasonably localized area. In such cases they are generally more efficient than a series of project specific EIAs. Regional EIA addresses issues that are addressed in project specific EIA but would further address issues that a project specific EIA will not address such as interactions amongst the project for land or water etc.

3) Sectoral EIA: Are used for design of sector investment programs. They are particularly suitable for reviewing sector investment alternatives, effect of sectoral policy changes and the cumulative impacts of many relatively small similar investments which do not merit individual project-specific EIA.

2.3   EIA Mandatory Study Activities

The FEPA EIA PROCEDURE (1995) makes EIA mandatory for the under listed activities:

1.   AGRICULURAL/AGRO-ALLIED ACTIVITIES
   a) Land development schemes covering an area of 500 hectares or more to bring forest land into agricultural production.

b) Agricultural programmes necessitating the resettlement of 100 families or more.

c) Development of agricultural estates covering an area of 500 hectares or more involving changes in types of agricultural use.

d) Wood/timber processing.

e) Saw milling.

2. FISHERIES

a) Construction of fishing harbor.

b) Harbor expansion involving an increase of 50 percent or more in fish landing capacity.

c) Land based agriculture projects accompanied by clearing of mangrove swamp forest covering an area of 50 hectares or more.

3. FORESTRY

a) Conversion of hill forest land use covering an area of 50 hectares or more.

b) Logging or conversion of forest land to other land use within the catchment area of reservoirs used for municipal water supply, irrigation, hydro-power generation or in areas adjacent to state and national parks and national marine parks.

c) Logging covering an area of 500 hectares or more.

d) Conversion of mangrove swamps for industrial, housing or agricultural use covering an area of 50 hectares or more

e) Clearing of mangrove swamps on islands adjacent to national marine parks.

4. INDUSTRY (MANUFACTURING)

   a) Chemical - where production capacity of each product or of combined products is greater than 100 tonnes/ day.
   b) Petrochemicals- all sizes.
   c) Non-ferrous – primary smelting.
      i. Aluminum – all sizes.
      ii. Copper – all sizes.
   d) Non-metallic
   i. Cement – for clinker throughout of 30 tonnes per hour and above.
   ii. Lime – 100 tonnes/day and above burnt lime rotary kiln or 50 tonnes/day and above vertical kiln.
   e) Iron and steel – require iron ore as raw materials for production greater than 100 tonnes/day or using scrap iron as raw materials for production greater than 200 tonnes per day.
   f) Shipyards – dead weight tonnages greater than 5000 tonnes.
   g) Pulp and paper – production capacity greater than 50 tonnes/ day.

5. FOOD BEVERAGES AND TOBACCO PROCESSING
   Construction of food processing plants.

6. INFRASTRUCTURE
   a) Construction of hospitals with outfall into beach fronts used for recreational purposes.

b) Industrial estate development for medium and heavy industries covering an area of 50 hectares or more.
c) Construction of expressway.
d) Construction of National highways.
e) Construction of new township.

7. PORTS
   a) Construction of ports.
   b) Port expansion involving an increase of 50 percent or more in handling.

8. HOUSING
   Housing development covering an area of 50 hectares or more.

9. AIRPORT
   a) Construction of Airport (having an airstrip of 2,500 meters or longer)
   b) Airstrip development in State and National Parks.

10. DRAINAGE AND IRRIGATION
    a) Construction of dams and man-made lakes and artificial enlargement of lakes with surface area of 200 hectares or more.
    b) Drainage of wetland, wildlife habitat or a virgin forest covering an area of 100 hectares or more.
    c) Irrigation schemes covering an area of 5,000 hectares or more.

      d) Construction of new routes.

      e) Construction of branch lines.

11.   TRANSPORTATION

      Construction of Mass Rapid Transport Projects.

12.   RESORT AND RECREATIONAL DEVELOPMENT

      a) Construction of coastal resort facilities or hotels with more than 80 rooms.

      b) Hill station resort or hotel development covering an area of 50 hectares or more.

      c) Development of tourist recreational facilities in national parks.

      d) Development of tourist or recreational facilities on islands in surrounding waters which may be declared as National Marine Parks.

13.   POWER GENERATION AND TRANSMISSION

      a) Construction of steam generated power station burning fossil fuel having a capacity of more than 10 mega-watts.

      b) Dams and hydroelectric power schemes with either or both of the following:

      c) Dams over 15 meters high and ancillary structures covering a total area in excess of 40 hectares.

      d) Construction of combined cycle power station.

      e) Construction of nuclear-fuelled power station.

14. PETROLEUM

    a) Oil and gas fields' development.

    b) Construction of off-shore, on-shore and overland pipelines.

    c) Construction of oil and gas separation, processing, handling and storage facilities.

    d) Construction of refineries.

    e) Construction of product depot for storage petrol, gas or diesel which are located within 3 kilometers of any commercial, industrial or residential areas and which have a combined storage capacity of 60,000 barrels or more.

15. MINING

    a) Mining of materials in new areas where the mining lease covers a total area in excess of 250 hectares.

    b) Ore processing, including concentrating for aluminium, copper, gold or titanium.

    c) Sand dredging involving an area of 50 hectares or more.

    d) Quarrying of sand stone, marble and decorative building stone within 3 kilometers of existing residential, commercial or industrial area, or any area for which a license permit or approval has been granted for residential, commercial or industrial development.

16. WASTE TREATMENT AND DISPOSAL

   16.1 Toxic and hazardous waste.
   a) Construction of incineration plant.
   b) Construction of recovery plant (off-site/on-site).
   c) Construction of waste treatment plant (off-site/ on-site).
   d) Construction of secure landfills facility.
   e) Construction of storage facility (off-site/on-site).

   16.2 Municipal solid waste
   a) Construction of incineration plant.
   b) Construction of composting plant.
   c) Construction of recovery/recycling plant.
   d) Construction of municipal solid waste landfills facility.
   16.3 Municipal sewage
   a) Construction of waste water treatment plant.
   b) Construction of outfall.

17. WATER SUPPLY
   a) Construction of dams, impounding reservoirs with surface area of 200 hectares or more.
   b) Ground water development for industrial agricultural or urban waste supply of greater than 4,500 cubic meters per day.

18. LAND RECLAMATION
   Coastal reclamation involving an area of 50 hectares or more.

19. BREWERY
   Construction of brewery plant.

The DPR EGASPIN (2002) listed the types of projects or activities as requiring EIA as follows:

1) All seismic operations.

2) Oil and gas field development, onshore, near shore, offshore and deep offshore.

3) Development well drilling.

4) Construction of crude oil production, tantaform and terminal facilities including FPSOS.

5) Laying of crude oil gas delivery line, flow line and pipeline in cumulative excess of 20km length and/or as determined by the Director of Petroleum Resources.

6) Hydrocarbon processing facilities

7) Oil refineries and petrochemicals.

8) Liquefied Natural Gas/Natural Gas Liquids/GC and Plants.

9) Liquefied Petroleum Gas (above 20,000 litres)

10) Blending plants.

11) Product filling station (combined capacity above 20,000 litres).

12) Construction of product depot with combined capacity of 50,000 bbls or more.

13) Construction of waste treatment or disposal facilities viz:

14) Waste water treatment plant.

15) Incineration process above 300kg/hr.

16) Engineer sanitary land filling.

17) Land farming/composting/ex-situ bio remediations in excess of 1.25km of land take.

18) Dredging activities of about 500m^2.

The World Bank EA source book listed the following projects/components as categories of activities that will require environmental assessment.

1) Aquaculture (large scale).

2) Dams and Reservoirs.

3) Electrical Transmission (large scale).

4) Forestry.

5) Industrial Plants (large scale) and Industrial Estates.

6) Irrigation and Drainage (large scale).

7) Land clearance and leveling.

8) Mineral Development (including oil and gas).

9) Pipelines (oil, gas and water).

10) Port and harbor development.

11) Reclamation and new land development.

12) Resettlement.

13) River Basin development.

14) Rural roads.

15) Thermal and Hydropower Development.

16) Tourism (large scale).

17) Transportation (airports, railways, roads, waterways).

18) Urban Development (large scale).

19) Urban water supply and sanitation (large scale).

20) Manufacture, transportation and use of pesticides or other hazardous and/or toxic materials.

21) Projects which pose serious accident risks.

From the list of activities requiring EIA as obtained in the FEPA, DPR and World Bank requirements, it is evident that all activities, processes, projects and actions that may have adverse and significant impacts on socio-cultural, physical, biological and chemical environment are obligated to undergo EIA studies prior to their implementation.

2.4 Resources Required for an EIA

Environmental assessments require interdisciplinary analysis and are therefore expected to be prepared by qualified multidisciplinary teams. The disciplines listed below are generally represented on the core team for any EIA as appropriate (World Bank EAOD).

1) A planner, social or natural scientist or environmental engineer as the Project Manager

(The Project Manager should necessarily have experience in preparing several EIAs. He or she must have management skills and sufficiently broad training and/or experience to be able to provide overall guidance and to integrate the findings of individual disciplines.

2) Ecologist and biologist (aquatic, marine or terrestrial specialization as appropriate).

3) Sociologist/anthropologist who has experience with communities similar to that of the project.

4) Geographer or geologist/hydrologist/soil scientist.

5) Urban or regional planner.

6) Agronomist, forest or land-use specialist

7) Fisheries scientist/biologist

8) Engineer with corresponding expertise, such as pollution control process engineer etc.

The core team needs to be supported by various specialists depending on the project and its setting. The table below shows some of the specialists that should be consulted.

Table2.1: Specialist Related to Environmental Assessment

Natural Resources	Sub Component	Specialist
Air	Air quality. Wind direction and speed, Precipitation/humidity, Temperature. Noise.	Air quality/pollution analyst, Air pollution control engineer. Meteorologist. Noise expert
Land	Land Capability Soil resources/structure Mineral resources Tectonic activity Unique features	Agronomist Soil engineer/Soil Scientist Civil engineer Geologist Geotechnical engineer Mineralogist Mining engineer Engineering geologist Seismologist
Water	Surface waters Groundwater regime Hydrologic balance Drainage/channel pattern Flooding Sedimentation	Hydrologist Water pollution control engineer Water quality/ pollution analyst Marine biologist/engineer Chemist Civil/sanitary engineer Hydro-geologist
Flora and Fauna	Environmentally sensitive areas: wetlands, marshes, wildlands, grassland etc Species inventory Biodiversity Ecosystem productivity Biogeochemical/nutrient cycling	Ecologist Forester Wildlife biologist Botanist Zoologist Conservationist
Human	Social Infrastructural Institutions Cultural characteristics Physiological and Psychological well-being Economic resources	Social anthropologist Sociologist Archaeologist Architect Social Planner Geographer Demographer

Source: World Bank EA Source Book.

Other relevant EIA resources are as shown below:

1) Analytical capabilities for field work, laboratory analysis, data processing and predictive modeling

2) Technical Guidelines provided by competent authorities such as Federal Ministry of Environment, Department of Petroleum Resources and the World Bank.

3) Administrative support for the day to day running of the EIA.

4) Institutional arrangement that provides for cross-functional inter-agency coordination (inter-agency coordination is crucial for effective EIA because environmental issues in their complexity and variety, are often inter-sectoral and regional, even international). The authority and responsibility to deal with them, to collect information, prepare plans, approve designs, issue permits, allocate resources, develop budgets, monitor progress and regulate activities is spread over a number of organization and agencies at all levels of government.

5) Funding: Funding is a critical element of an effective EIA, funding is required for the EIA study and implementation of the mitigation measures. The cost of EIA however varies with the type, size and complexity of the project, the characteristics of its physical, socio-cultural and institutional setting. Meanwhile, EIA preparation cost rarely exceeds one percent of the total capital cost of the project and could be less than that. The cost of

implementing mitigation measures may not exceed 10 percent of total project with 3 to 5 percent being common (World Bank EA Source Book). This estimate is not cast in stone as a host of factors could potentially affect the cost of executing an EIA.

6) Effective monitoring and Enforcement: Regulatory monitoring and enforcement powers are needed to ensure that mitigation measures proffered in the EIA are implemented throughout the project lifecycle.

2.5 Characteristic features of Standard EIA

An EIA that must pass the litmus test of standard EIA must meet the following requirements
1. Must be comprehensive
2. Detailed, concise and easy to comprehend
3. Consistent with established regulations and standards
4. Follow standard processes and procedures
5. Establish baseline condition in qualitative and quantitative terms
6. Establish interaction between project activities and environmental impact i.e. activities- receptor interaction.
7. Provide quantitative and qualitative impact assessment
8. Predictive
9. Contains implementable post EIA monitoring programmes
10. Show evidence of interagency and stakeholders coordination and consultation.

Chapter Three

EIA PROCEDURES AND INTERRELATED ACTIVITIES

This chapter details the step by step procedures of undertaking EIA for projects as well as activities required in line

The EIA procedures will be discussed in line with the requirement of the Federal Ministry of Environment (FMEV) and Department of Petroleum Resources (DPR) Requirements EIA regulations and guidelines. The Federal Ministry of Environment procedure identified 10 procedures as shown below:

Procedure 1: Project Notification/Project proposal

Procedure 2: Site verification

Procedure 3: Screening

Procedure 4: Scoping/TOR Approval

Procedure 5: EIA studies

Procedure 6: Submission of Draft EIA Report

Procedure 7: Review

- In-house review
- Public review (21 working days)
- Technical review/panel review
- Mediation

Procedure 8: Submission of final EIA Report

Procedure 9: Certification

Procedure 10: Follow up activities

- Monitoring
- EMP implementation
- Audit
- Decommissioning.

The procedures identified above can be graphically represented as shown in the flow chart in fig 3.1below:

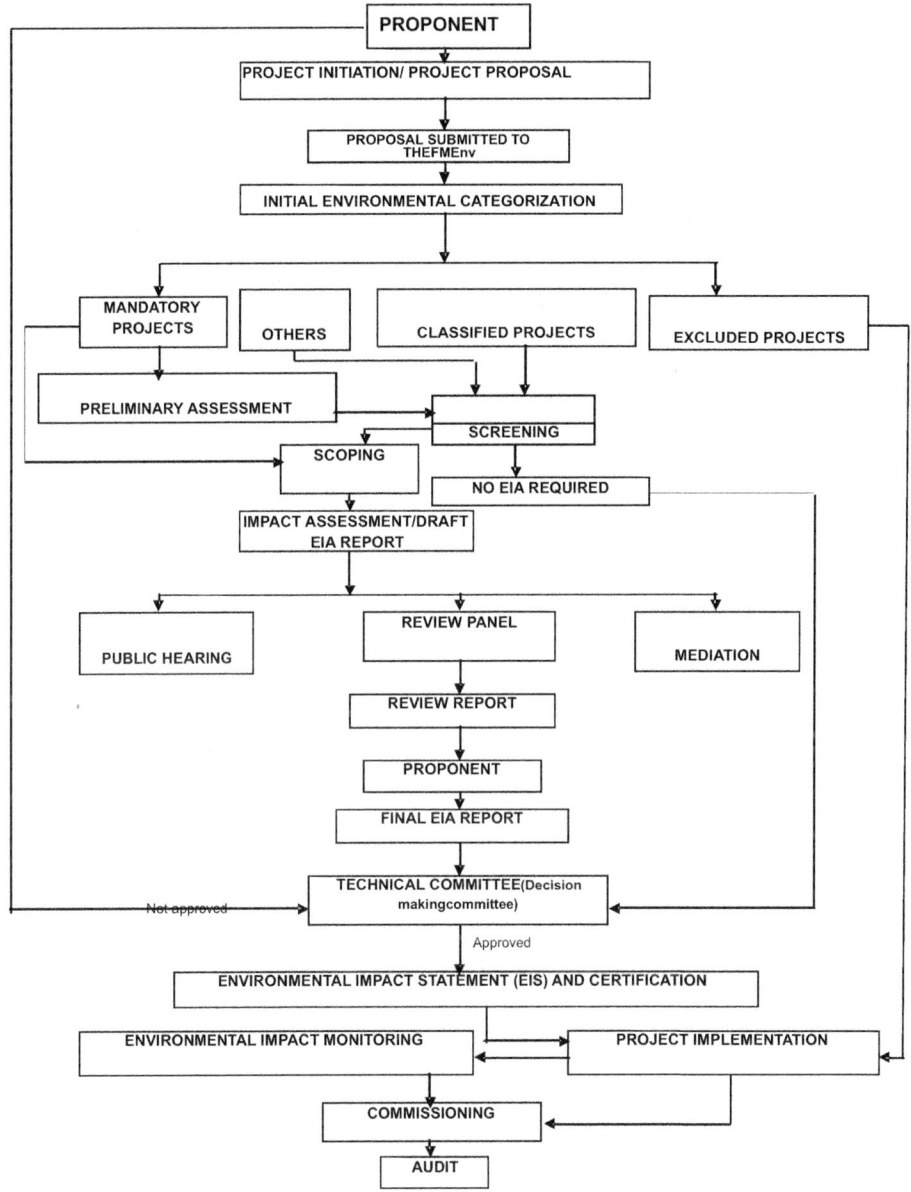

The DPR EIA Guidelines recognizes a systematic process with nine (9) procedures shown below.

Procedure 1: DPR is notified by a proponent of the project or activity as conceptualized and an initial assessment/environmental screening exercise is carried out to determine impact significance of the project alternatives

Procedure 2: A preliminary assessment of impacts (PIAR) focused on the selected project option is carried out.

Procedure 3: Scoping/TOR approval for detailed EIA study if PIAR identifies potentially significant impacts, if not the project activity may proceed with appropriate mitigation measures.

Procedure 4: Submission of Draft EIA report following detailed EIA study.

Procedure 5: Technical review of the Draft EIA report by DPR and issuance of provisional approval.

Procedure 6: Submission of final EIA report at the end of detailed engineering design.

Procedure 7: DPR issues final EIA approval.

Procedure 8: Implementation of mitigation measures (construction and operational phase).

Procedure 9: Post-EIA monitoring and auditing programme implementation.

Fig 3.2 below shows a graphical representation of the procedures discussed above

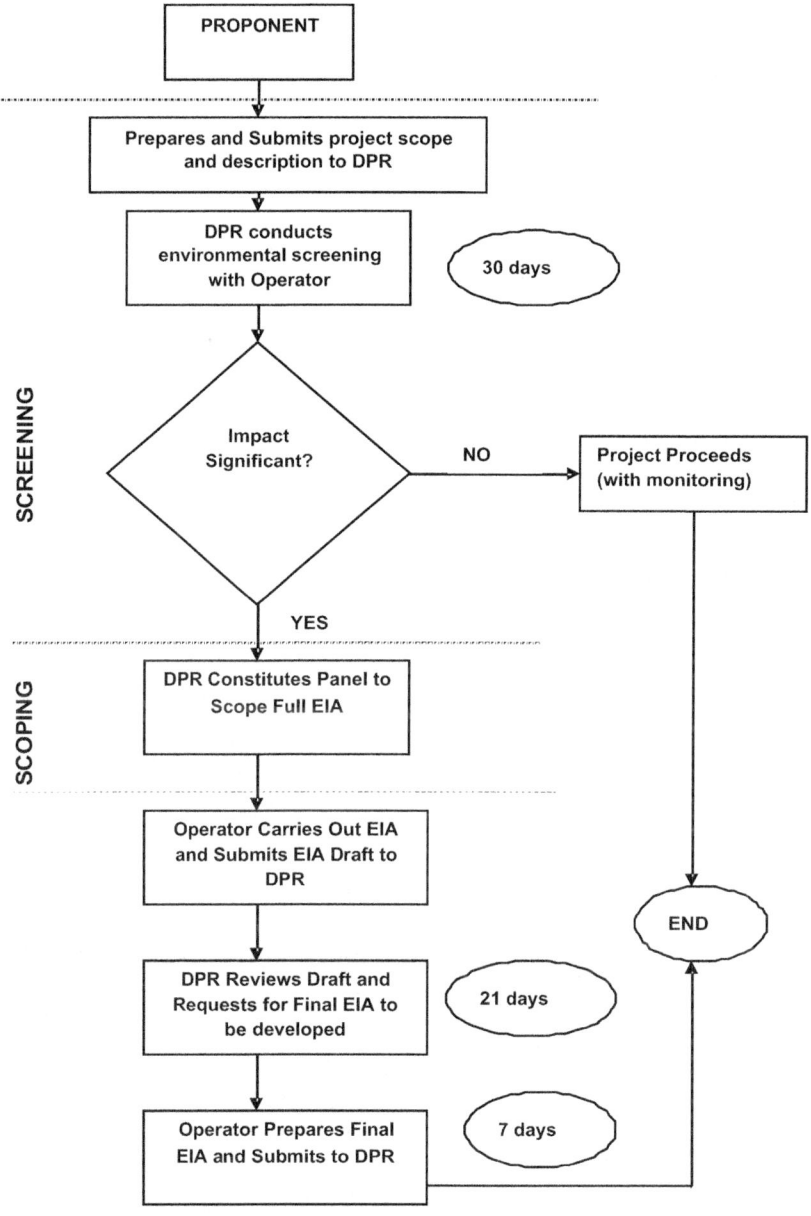

Fig 3.2 : DPR EIA Processes

3.1 Project Notification/Project proposal

The operator/proponent having made a preliminary investment decisions on project development makes known its intension by notifying the regulatory bodies (FMEV or/and DPR) as applicable, providing relevant information on the description of the proposed project. The Federal Ministry of Environment requires that proponents in addition to making formal notification should duly complete the "EIA NOTIFICATION FORM" made available upon the payment of the prescribed application fee. Submission of project proposal is the starting point of the EIA process. The regulatory bodies officially register the project proposal and issue a registration number as well as acknowledge receipt.

3.2 Site Verification

This is the reconnaissance survey conducted by the Federal Ministry of Environment to have first hand information on the existing environmental settings at the proposed project site. The visit helps the Ministry to visualize the current ecological and environmental conditions at the proposed location and adjoining areas. Importantly also, it is to enable the ministry verify whether the proponent had illegally commenced the development of the project/action prior to registration of the project and execution of the EIA study.

3.3 Screening

Screening implies the evaluation of the environmental and socio-economic impacts of the proposed project and alternatives in order to determine whether the project under consideration would have potentially significant environmental, social and health impacts.

Preliminary screening of projects is normally carried out by the regulatory agencies having the responsibility to determine EIA category that a project belongs. For instance in Nigeria, the Federal Ministry of Environment conducts an Initial Environmental Examination (IEE)/ screening and assigns the project or activity into a category I, II or III upon receipt of project proposal and registration of the project.

Category I are projects for which full scale EIA is required i.e. EIA is mandatory.
Category II are projects for which a partial EIA will be required.

Category III are projects which are expected to have essential beneficial impacts on the environment and as such EIA is not required but the Ministry will issue an Environmental Impact Statement (EIS)

The World Bank EA Operational Directive uses screening to categorize projects into categories A, B, C or D based upon the nature, magnitude and sensitivities of environmental issues.

Category A – Environmental Assessment is normally required as the project may have diverse and significant impacts.

Category B – More limited environmental analysis is appropriate, as the project may have specific environmental effect.

Category C – Environmental analysis is normally unnecessary.

Category D – Environmental projects for which separate Environment Assessment may not be required as environment would be a major focus of project preparation.

3.3.1 Stakeholders Joint Screening

Once a project falls into the category requiring environmental assessment such as category I, public/stakeholders screening workshop is conducted to identify the potentially significant impacts the project may produce on the environment. This screening is a high-level evaluation of potential environmental, social and health impacts to inform business decision-making. It is aimed at determining if the project may have potentially significant environmental, social and health impacts and the need for further impact assessment.

The screening procedure involves the use of checklist or other tools which relates a list of environmental settings and possible environmental impact indicators. The screening identifies activities which are likely to occur during the principal phases of project development and the environmental aspects with possible interaction with the physical, chemical, biological, anthropogenic, aesthetic, health, social, economic etc. in which environmental effects can be expected.

The screening exercise is normally conducted in a workshop where the proponent pull together Subject Matter Experts (SMEs) in relevant disciplines and stakeholders which includes representatives of the project communities and the relevant regulatory agencies to evaluate the interactions between the proposed action/projects and the environment to determine whether the impact will be potentially significant or not. It helps in identifying whether it would be positive or negative. A yes, no or may be answer to the questions that bother on the possibility of impact as shown in table 3.1that is provided on the corresponding column. A yes or maybe answer indicates that the subject should be in the scope of the EIA study. Upon the completion of the screening exercise and environmental screening report indicating whether there is need for scoping or not is prepared and submitted to the appropriate regulatory agencies. Environmental screening of proposed project is performed to determine the appropriate type of environmental analysis, based on the nature, potential magnitude, and sensitivities of the issues. Shown below is a sample checklist for screening a project.

Table 3.1: Sample screening checklist/matrix

S/N	Category/question	Responses (No/Yes/Unknown)	Impact Significance (Potentially significant, not potentially significant or insurmountable impacts)	Explanation/discussion note
1	Social and Cultural Resources: Existing Cultural Practices impact question	Responses are provided by the participants	Alternative 1 Alternative 2	Alternative 1 Alternative 2
2	Hazards: Geological impact question			
3	Hazards: Climatic-			
4	Hazards: Oceanographic-			
5	Hazards from Wastes:			
6	Solid Wastes:			
7	Hazardous Wastes:			
8	Solid Wastes Management:			
9	Surface and Ground Water Quality:			
10	Hydrology and Water Quality:			
11	Natural Resource Depletion:			
12	Ambient Noise change:			
13	Noise pollution:			
14	Economic conditions:			

15	Population, Housing and Employment:			
16	Occupational Health and safety:			
17	Public Health:			
18	Community Infrastructure?			
19	Transportation and Traffic:			
20	Political unrest and Reputation/Liability:			
21	Reputation and Liability:			

Screening is to ensure that the adequate attention is devoted to the environmental aspects of proposed project from the very outset of the project cycle, meant to identify as much as possible, the key environmental issues and to determine the type of environmental analysis which is needed so that those issues can be addressed effectively in the EIA scope, project, planning, design and appraisal.

The benefits of screening include the following:
- Environmental concerns will be identified early in the project planning phase.
- It build regulators confidence and facilitate timely approval of project permit applications.
- It promotes project compliance with regulatory requirements.
- The proponent will better appreciate the interactions between project and the physical and socio-economic environment with the potential impacts;
- Boost community participation and support

From the foregoing discussions, it is clear that screening/preliminary overview assessment project is critical in determining the need for an environmental impact assessment for a project/activity and degree of details required for the study.

3.4   Preliminary Assessment of Impacts (PIAR)

Preliminary Impact Assessment is conducted at the end of concept selection studies and focuses on the selected project option per DPR EIA requirement to determine the significance of the potential and associated environmental impact of the selected project option. The approval of the PIAR forms the basis for the approval of the project conceptual engineering design.

PIAR can be likened to a desktop EIA where no field sampling exercise is conducted. The preliminary assessment of impact carried out with the review of the project activities, existing literature and environmental studies providing background environmental information around the project area. Impact Assessment matrix used for impact assessment in detailed EIA study is used to evaluate the potential impact of the proposed action/project. If no potentially significant impacts that would necessitate detailed EIA study, DPR issues approval for the project to proceed with recommended mitigation measures and post EIA monitoring. If the PIAR identifies potentially significant impacts that justify the need for further impact assessment, a detailed EIA study shall be conducted by proponent based on DPR recommendations on the Terms of Reference/ Scope of work (TOR/SOW) submitted for the detailed EIA study. PIAR interfaces between screening and scoping i.e. PIAR is conducted before the scoping exercise.

The Federal Ministry of Environment EIA re-interpreted that it is a process of screening and categorization of projects using criteria such as magnitude, extent or scope, risks significance, duration. Frequency and location of project is conducting preliminary overview assessment of impacts of the project and is adequate to provide information on the need or otherwise for detailed Impact Assessment Study.

3.5 Scoping

Upon receipt of screening report by the Ministry and also based on the findings of the environmental screening Report, the proponent carry out all significant exercise to ensure that all significant impacts and reasonable alternatives are addressed in the EIA study. Before any analysis commences, it is important to determine the appropriate level of study and to indentify the issues and concerns that will be the focus of the study efforts i.e. to determine what issues are important and deserve detailed and intense study. The significance of scoping includes:

1) Defines issues that should be addressed in the EIA study.

2) Ensures that no significant issue of concern is left out in the study.

3) Builds integration and coordination among the stakeholders.

4) Helps in identification of relevant regulations and permits.

5) Provides clarification on project information.

6) Builds stakeholders confidence in the EIA process.

7) Provides the necessary information to aid development of the terms of reference (TOR) and Scope of work (SOW) of the project impact assessment

Scoping exercise is normally conducted in a workshop setting with the proponent representatives from key departments such as environment, public affairs and project management, regulatory agencies, environmental consultants, community and non-governmental organizations.

The focus of discussions at the scoping workshop is largely influenced by the findings of the screening exercise and at the end of the scoping exercise. The Terms of Reference/Scope of Work (TOR/SOW) for the EIA study is prepared and submitted to the appropriate regulatory agencies for approvals. The approved TOR/SOW shall form the basis with which the EIA study shall be undertaken.

Meanwhile there is currently no specific requirement by the FME_{nv} and DPR EIA regulations that mandates proponents to organize a public scoping meeting defining relevant stakeholders to participate in the scoping exercise. This makes it possible for proponents to use its discretion to conduct an in-house scoping or public scoping meeting. Nevertheless, participation of the relevant ministry and government departments often enhances the process of approval of the TOR.

It is important to note here that the effectiveness of an EIA begins with the quality of the screening and scoping exercises.

3.6   Detailed Impact Assessment

According to the English Thesaurus, the word "assess" means to appraise, compute, estimate, rate, value, assign, determine, fix and impose. When an assessment is conducted, the essence is to make estimation in order to provide sound judgment in a given circumstance.

Once the TOR/SOW is approved by the regulatory agencies such as FME_{nv} and/or DPR, the stage is set for assessment study to be conducted for the proposed project action. This stage of the EIA Procedure is critical for it is the time to determine and establish the baseline environmental conditions at the project site and make predictions on possible impacts based on the expected interactions between project activities and the environmental components.

Impact Assessment Study involves coordination between and among different stakeholders both internally (with the organization) and externally (government and the public). The process of the study commence with the proponent putting in place consultant selection and contract award process. These processes vary from organization to organization. The common goal is to select a qualified and competent environmental consultant company that is capable of meeting the objective of the EIA and delivery on the requirements of the EIA TOR/SOW.

Within the organization, coordination is normally between the environment department, project team, public affairs group and legal department. External coordination and consultation will be driven by the obligation on the part of the proponent to obtain relevant regulatory approval and participations. The schedule for the field sampling exercise would necessarily be approved by the regulators. The acceptance of field sampling schedule is communicated with the nomination of their representative(s) to participate in the exercise in order to enable them perform the regulatory and supervisory roles and functions.

Consultation is also required with the stakeholders' communities. Formal and informal engagements are conducted in order to involve the communities in critical stages of the EIA process. For a field sampling exercise to be successful, cooperation and support of the host communities must be obtained. This is not only critical for the EIA; it is as well decisive for the success of the project. Once all consultations are consolidated and consummated, the plan for the mobilization of the field sampling exercise would be firmed upon. The under-listed activities are the basic components of EIA impact assessment study:

1)   Field sampling/ field data gathering exercise.
2)   Laboratory analysis.
3)   Data analysis and interpretation.
4)   Description of the proposed project.
5)   Impact identification, assessment and prediction.
6)   Development of appropriate mitigation measures.
7)   Development of the Environmental Management Plan.
8)   Report writing (items 3-7 above).
9)   Report production

3.7   Draft EIA Report Preparation and Submission

Following detailed EIA studies, the proponent is required by the FME_{nv} and the DPR EIA regulations to submit Draft EIA report for their review and approvals. All process analysis, findings and recommendations are presented in the report to provide information upon which decisions will be made on the environmental sustainability or otherwise of the project.

Meanwhile, in a two-season (dry and wet seasons) EIA study; a progress report is submitted after the first season sampling while the draft report is completed after the second season is conducted. The regulations do not recognize the progress report and as such could be ignored by proponents and make the draft EIA submission after the second season sampling exercise.

Prior to submitting the draft report to the regulator(s), the proponent is expected to coordinate with the consultant to ensure its correctness and accuracy, it is the responsibility of the proponent to ensure that the report satisfies regulatory requirements for an EIA study.

The Federal Ministry of Environment EIA regulation requires 15 bound copies of the draft report to be submitted to it for review. The FME_{nv} has 4 review stages to complete the review process as shown below:

a)   In-house review
b)   Public display (21 working day)
c)   Technical review/ panel review/public hearing
d)   Mediation.

Upon receipt of the draft report, the FME_{nv} sets in motion, the review process by first going through the report and subjecting it to in-house review by the EIA division to gain good understanding of the report. Then would the ministry coordinate with the proponent to make publication in the national print and electronic media announcement on the public display of the draft EIA report for 21 working days to enable the public particularly the stakeholders (Communities, NGO$_s$ etc.) review the report and provide the feedback. Venue of display include among others; the Local Government Area Office of the project location, the State Environmental Protection Agency/ Ministry of Environment Office and the Federal Ministry of Environment Office in Abuja. Following the public display exercise, the Ministry will constitute a technical team drawn from the Universities and amongst seasoned EIA Practitioners to review the draft report and harmonize the different comments arising from the public hearing exercise.

Panel review/hearing involves the assembling of some persons with known or demonstrable experience and expertise in EIA (Panel of experts) to elicit their views. Included in the review process is mediation which provides for arbitration on areas where there are conflicts of interest. It is the time to settle issue of disagreement in the EIA report. The degree to which all issues are resolved from environmental, technical, community, best practices and regulatory stand point would be the basis for the issuance of provisional approval or otherwise by the ministry.

The Department of Petroleum Resources (DPR) review process is different from the FMEnv process, the major difference is that DPR review process does not involve public review; all reviews are done internally, nevertheless. There exists a mechanism through which community and other stakeholders concerns are addressed and relevant in determining the issuance of provisional approval and feedback to the proponent.

3.8   Final EIA Report Preparation and Submission

FME$_{NV}$ and DPR provisional approval normally will provide comments on their observations and position on the draft EIA report. It identifies issues to be addressed by the proponent in the final EIA reports. Once these issues are addressed satisfactorily by the proponent, the final EIA report (2 to 5 copies) can be made available to DPR and FME$_{NV}$ respectively.

Meanwhile, a key requirement for the submission of the final EIA report to DPR is that the detailed engineering design of the project must have been completed or frozen and approved before the final EIA is submitted. The purpose is to ensure that all associated and potential impacts of the project processes and description as depicted in the detailed engineering drawing are addressed by the final EIA report.

The FME$_{NV}$ EIA Guideline requires that the final EIA report be submitted to the ministry within 6 months of the receipt of the Ministry's comments on the draft EIA failing which the ministry may request for a raised and upgraded EIA report.

Upon submission of satisfactory final EIA report addressing issues raised in the provisional approval, the final EIA approval is issued by the regulatory bodies as applicable.

The FME$_{NV}$ issues an Environmental Impact Statement (EIS) stating the conditions of approval or disapproval of a project. The condition of approval is issued following the submission of a satisfactory final EIA report. The Ministry in consultation with the proponent set a number of conditions which may provide for the establishment of a follow-up programme (mitigation, compliance and monitoring plan) with specified tasks to be undertaken in the construction, operational and decommissioning phases of the development. Penalties as stipulated in the EIA Decree No 86 of 1992 may be invoked for failure to adhere to the condition of approval.

3.9   Post- EIA Activities

After certification, the proponent may proceed to implement the project in accordance with all the stipulated mitigation measures as contained in the final EIA Report. The final EIA approval confers the proponent with the authority to commence construction activities. At this stage, the decisions have been made on the implementation of the project considering the environment, ecological and socio-economic sustainability of the project.

Nevertheless, the effectiveness of the EIA is determined by the effectiveness of the post-EIA activities listed below:
I.   Monitoring
ii.   EMP implementation
iii. Auditing.
During the implementation of the project, the regulatory bodies shall monitor the progress of the project from site preparation to commissioning in order to ensure compliance with regulatory requirements and all stipulated measures in the EIA report. They engage in monitoring activities and systematic collection of

environmental data through repetitive measurement in order to determine the effectiveness of the mitigation measures in the EIA report and provide basis for early warnings in case there are deviations from environmental controls that are in place to mitigate negative impacts to the environment. Two key monitoring are applicable here, viz:

a)   Effect monitoring

b)   Compliance monitoring

Per the FMEnv Environmental Impact Assessment Procedural Guidelines (1995), the above stated procedures covering project proposal, Initial Environmental Examination (IEE), Screening, Scoping, the EIA Study Review, Decision making, Monitoring and Auditing. is summarized as follows

- *Project proponent outlines information required in the "EIA Notification Form" and payment of application fee of N10,000.00 (ten thousand naira only). The Ministry will register the project proposal and issue a registration number to the proponent.*

- *The Ministry will carry out Initial Environmental Examination (IEE) and assign the project into a Category I, II or III Project. Site verification may be undertaken.*

- *The Proponent carries out a scoping exercise to ensure that all significant impacts and reasonable alternatives are addressed.*
- *The proponent conducts EIA field data gathering, analysis, and report preparation*

- *The Proponent submits fifteen (15) copies of a Draft EIA Report to the Ministry for review.*

- *The Ministry shall charge a prescribed fees of N250,000.00 (two hundred and fifty thousand naira only) processing fee for processing the EIA document*

- · *The Ministry evaluates the Draft EIA Report and coordinate public hearing/review of the report*

- *The Project Proponent will submit the Final EIA Report to the Ministry within six (6) months of receipt of the comments from the Ministry.*

- · *The Minister issues Final EIA Approval of the Final EIA report*

- *The Minister considers/approve issuance of an Environmental Impact Statement (EIS).*

- *The Minister shall issue a Certificate upon receipt of an EIS. The Ministry shall publish its decision in a manner by which members of the public shall be notified in accordance with the Act.*

- *The Proponent shall proceed to implement the project after Certification.*

- *The Ministry shall carry out Impact Mitigation Monitoring (IMM) of the project during the implementation to ensure compliance with stipulated mitigation measures specification.*

- *The Ministry shall carry out the periodic assessment (auditing) of the positive and negative impacts of the project, to help improve the EIA Process*

Chapter Four

DESCRIPTION OF
THE ENVIRONMENT

> *This chapter presents information on the methodologies for environmental characterization with practical guidance on field data gathering, laboratory analysis and data interpretation.*

This is the description of the current condition of the environment as it exists prior to project development/execution or operations. Emphasis is placed on the environmental components that are of significant importance to the proposed project, detailed information is provided on the environmental setting at the immediate environment of the project and Area of Potential Project Influence (APPI). The description provides scientific data that serves as basis for comparing future environment data in order to establish the extent to which there post-project environmental conditions.

Environmental description also provides the basis for impact Assessment and prediction. For instance, description of the environment provides information on the ecologically sensitive areas in and around the proposed site, this helps in appreciating the sensitivity of the environmental receptors at the area and as such the potential environmental effect of the project activities. A clear and detailed description of the existing environment is provided in qualitative and quantitative terms.

The description shall include but is not limited to the under-listed environmental components including natural resources as contained in the Physical, Biological, chemical and Socio-cultural environment.

i. Physical environment:
    a. Geographical location
    b. Climate and meteorology
    c. Hydrology and water quality
    d. Topography
    e. Soil
    f. Oceanography etc.

ii. Biological environment:
    a. Flora and fauna (biodiversity)
    b. Ecologically sensitive areas
    c. Micro-organisms
    d. Plankton
    e. Macrophyte
    f. Species of commercial importance etc.

iii. Chemical environment
    a) Soil/water/air chemical composition
    b) Organic/inorganic elements
    c) Environmental quality parameters
    d) Chemical and geochemical reactions etc
    e) Contamination and pollution

iv. Socio-cultural environment:
   a. Population
   b. Demography
   c. Land use
   d. Planned development
   e. Employment and income
   f. Public health
   g. Culture and custom
   h. Infrastructural development etc.

In addition to above, the environmental description should include the potential environmental contaminants in the physical, chemical and biological components and the capacity of the ecological system, to assimilate possible pollutants/contaminants resulting from the proposed development or activity.

In order to provide empirical description of the environment, studies are conducted to carry out an evaluation of the ecological and environmental processes. Evaluation which is the systematic acquisition and assessment of information to provide useful feedback about a phenomenon involves the deployment of research methodologies to obtaining useful data that provide details of the environmental studies carried out in the project area.

The information to characterize the environment are obtained during the under listed activities:
   1)   Literature review
   2)   Field data gathering

3)   Laboratory analyses

4)   Data analysis and interpretation

4.1   Literature Review

One of the most important early steps in environmental description is literature review carried out to identify related research/studies, findings and body of knowledge that provide information/data on the physic-chemical, biological and socio-economic environment of the study area. These data can be in form of maps, reports, journals, research paper etc. and may be obtained from academic institutions, governmental ministries/departments/agencies, research institutions, multinational organizations e.g. International oil companies, donor agencies and Non-Governmental Organizations (NGO), internet among others.

The Environmental Consultant is expected to consult relevant agencies to obtain the required information e.g. projects requiring excavation or tunneling or causing changes in drainage pattern would require an understanding of the basic physiography and topography and the underlying geology of the site or the area, the analyst should obtain relevant literature from the appropriate government departments e.g. such as the Nigerian Geological and Remote Sensing Agency. Topographical maps could be obtained from the Federal office of survey as well as relevant institutions. Alternatively, relevant literature materials that describe the environmental condition within a given ecological zone in Nigeria could be obtained from the Federal Ministry of Environmental and the Department of Petroleum Resources (If the project is oil and gas related), also the proponent may have a repository of literature materials that would be useful in characterizing the environment.

With relevant materials and data, the analyst can generate background information that would form part of the description of the different components of the environment (Land, water, air and human). Where there are variations in the literature information on a particular subject, a time series or trend analysis is presented with relation to the current findings derived from field data gathering exercise.

4.2   Field Data Gathering

This is also known as field sampling or field investigations. It is a critical activity in the EIA study that is often neglected in the EIA discussions. Data that will be documented are derived from the samples that have been collected at the project environment. Data gathering activities are carried out to collect, verify and update information on the environmental attributes of the study area, if the sampling premises is defective, the analytical indices will be misleading. It must be noted that the data collected during EIA study forms the basis on which the post-EIA, data will be measured, even though there are standards and regulatory limits for environmental data, a sampling strategy that is not representative of the environment would mislead the judgment of impact assessment and mess up the EIA report. For instance, if sampling is not conducted in areas where impacts are expected to occur, impact predictions and judgment would be on wrong assumptions.

4.2.1 Sampling Design Concepts and Terms
(a) Population

Target population is the set of all units that comprise the items of interest in a scientific study, that is, the population about which the decision maker wants to be able to draw conclusions. The sampled population is that part of the target population that is accessible and available for sampling. For example, the target population may be defined as surface soil in a residential yard, and the sampled population may be areas of soil in that yard not covered by structures or vegetation. Ideally, the sampled population and the target population are the same. If they are not, then professional judgment is used to verify that data drawn from the sampled population is appropriate for drawing conclusions about the target population.

(b) Sampling unit

This is also referred to as Experimental unit, and is defined as a single section selected to research and gather statistics of the whole. For example, when studying a group of college students, a single student could be a sampling unit

Sampling unit is a member of the population that may be selected for sampling, such as individual trees, or a specific volume of air or water. It is important for study planners to be very specific when defining a sampling unit's characteristics with respect to space and time. A sampling unit should detail the specific components of a particular environmental media. Some environmental studies have distinct sampling units such as trees, fish, or drums of waste material.

(c) Sampling

Sampling can be defined as the process of selecting units from a population of interest so that by studying the sample we may fairly generalize our results back to the population from which they were chosen. We collect samples on the environmental components of interest such as surface water, soil, sediment, air, at given points in order to generate information that represents that environmental component using specific analytical methods.

4.3   Pre field sampling activities

Prior to mobilization for field data gathering exercise. there are certain pre-sampling activities that should be conducted if the field sampling exercise would achieve its objectives:

I.   Reconnaissance survey/ pre-field investigation visit.

II.   Delineation of the study area.

III.   Development of the sampling plan.

IV.   Pre-mobilization logistics, meetings and consultation.

V.   Field investigation.

a)   Reconnaissance Survey/ Pre-field Investigation Visit.

This is a visit conducted to have an understanding of the general layout of the environmental settings at the site prior to conducting the field sampling exercise. It provides the opportunity for a visual assessment of the study area as this knowledge is useful in shaping decisions that would be made on the sampling design, methodology and approach.

An over-flight of the study area can be conducted to have aerial photographs taken and record some important habitat features such as drainage pattern, land use/ land cover etc. The study area can also be accessed by boat or by land to ground truth in order to verify information that is satellite images.

The information gathered during the pre-field investigation visit would be synthesized with those made available by the proponent to aid in the design of an effective sampling strategy.

b)   Delineation of the study Area

The study area is more often not limited to the immediate environment of the project site, it could cover geographical area to which the impact may extend. This depends on the nature and scope of the proposed project.

The boundaries of the study area for assessment should be specified including any adjacent or remote areas, this will be considered and accommodated in the EIA TOR/ SOW and sampling map .

The delineation of the study area would involve the delineation of the impact zone and the buffer zone, once this is successfully done decision on the sampling rationale and strategy will be enhanced to achieving a successful sampling exercise.

c)   Development of the sampling plan

The sampling plan provides the guidance for the sampling exercise. It is developed consisted with the EIA scope of work and regulatory requirement.

Meanwhile, sampling design/ plan/ strategy is based on a number of considerations which among others include: anticipated project environmental aspects, habitat-type, hydrology and drainage pattern, topography, wind direction, surface current direction, bottom current direction, relativity to project site, settlement pattern and distribution, the media to sample, parameters of interest etc.

While there are no hard rules on the sampling methodology to adopt for EIA sampling, there is a common requirement that the EIA sampling should be representative of the environment. How representative the samples are is best determined by employing tested sampling methods some of which are identified below:

a.   Simple random sampling

b.   Systematic random sampling

c.   Cluster (area) random sampling

d.   Multi-stage sampling (combination of sampling methods).

Listed above are the make up probability sampling method which utilizes some form of random selection that assures that the different units of the population have equal probability of being chosen.

However, there may be some circumstances where probability sampling method is not feasible, practical or theoretically sensible, then we consider a wide range of non-probabilistic alternatives which can be classified into:

a.   Accidental, haphazard or convenience sampling

b.   Purposive sampling.

In designing, the sampling plan for EIA study, a single sampling method may not be adequate to support the study, there may have to be a combination of two or more sampling methodologies.

In designing sampling rationale, several factors are taken into consideration to ensure that the project potential environmental zone of influence is adequately covered. The scope and activities will largely influence decisions on sampling design and sampling rationale, the environmental setting where the project will be sited is also a major factor that will influence decisions of sampling design. This suggests that there is no hard and fast rule on sampling design, the guiding philosophy is that the sampling design should be such that adequately and sufficiently represents and covers the project zone of influence.

The number of sampling stations to be established for a given study will largely depend on the factors identified above.

The establishment of sampling stations/ points and the number of such stations per given environmental component such as soil surface, water sediment, vegetation etc. would be enhanced by incorporation of best sampling strategies that is in alignment with regulatory requirement, this will greatly promote the achievement of the objectives of the sampling exercise.

In general, the following recommendations are key for a sampling design to be effective and acceptable.

1)   Regulatory requirements and industry best practices and standards must be considered in designing the study methodology

2)   It should be consistent with the recommendations of the screening and scoping reports

3)   The study should adequately surround the project area with sufficient butter to capture the extreme boundaries of the environmental influence the project may have.

Sampling plans are usually represented in sampling maps that is, designed based on the foregoing consideration and are properly geo-referenced in the coordinate system using GIS capabilities.

These considerations form what is referred to as sampling rationale which explains the reasoning behind proposed sample locations, number of samples, types of analyses, etc. For example the physical environmental setting and the area coverage of the proposed project location will influence the number of samples to factors that will influence decision on sample station establishment include: project scope and activities, anticipated releases and emission from project, environmental sensitivity of the project zone of influence, relative distance of population area to project location, land use around project site etc.

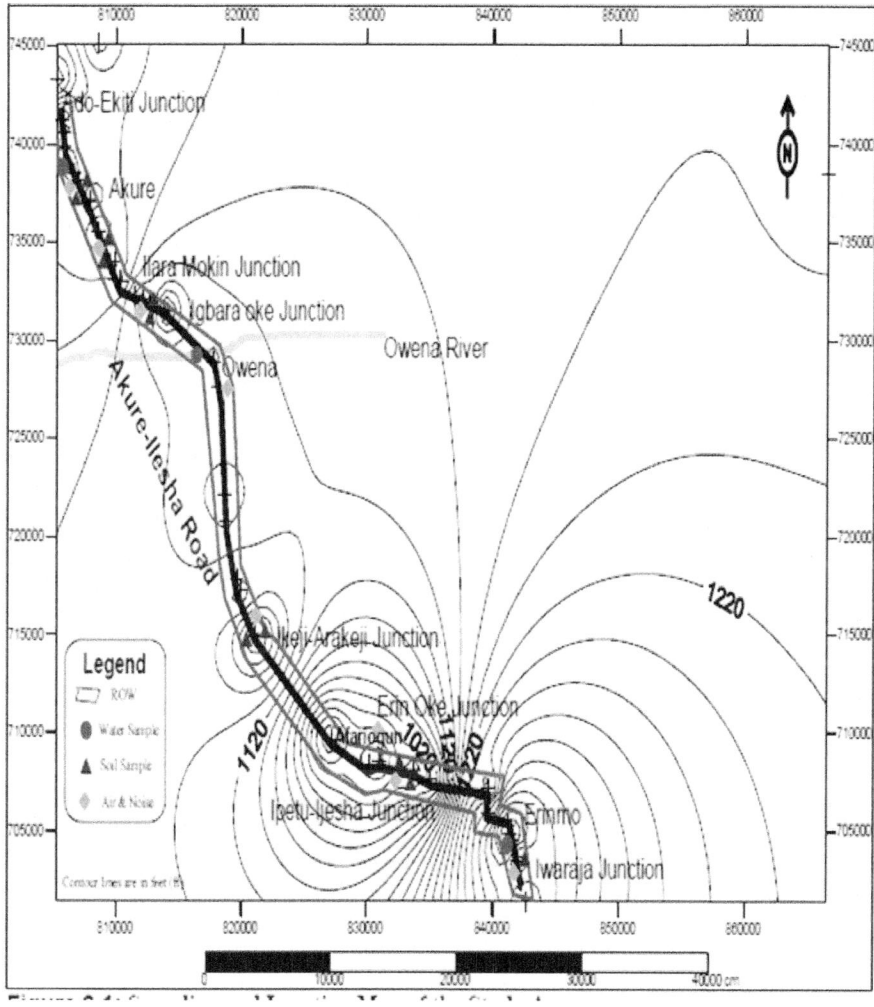

Fig 4.1: A road construction sampling map adapted from Ilesa-Akure Road EIA Report

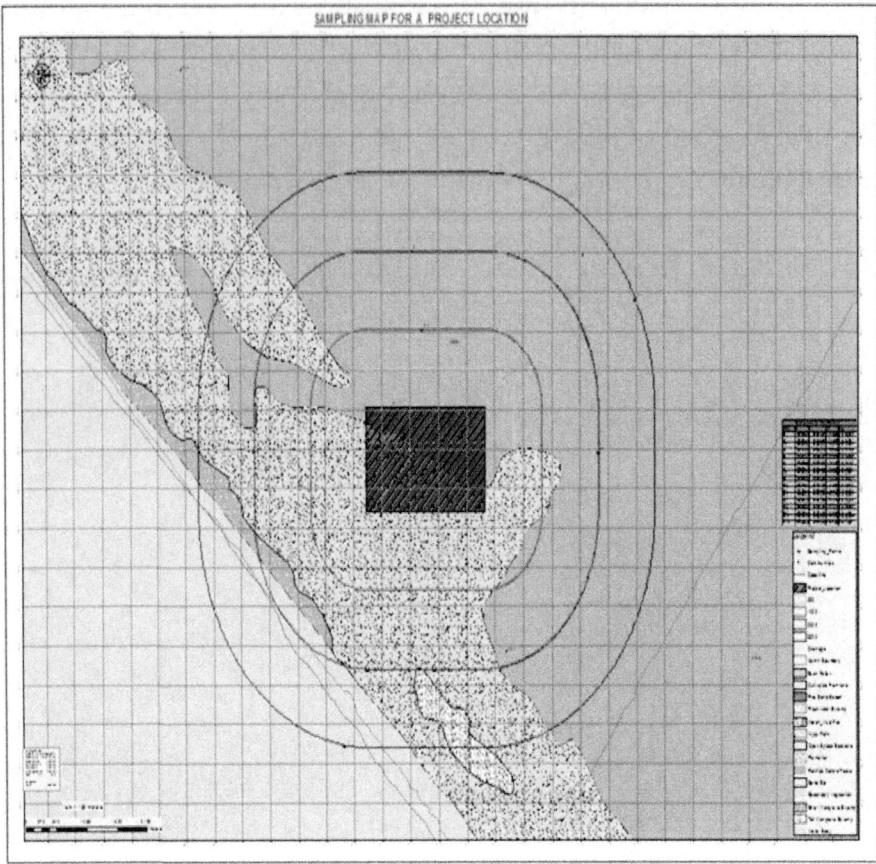

Fig 4.2: Typical sampling Map showing the sampling points and coordinates (Detail information on the map is shown on the legend)

The sampling distribution that derives from the sampling rationale shown in the sampling map can be outlined as shown in fig 4.3 below:

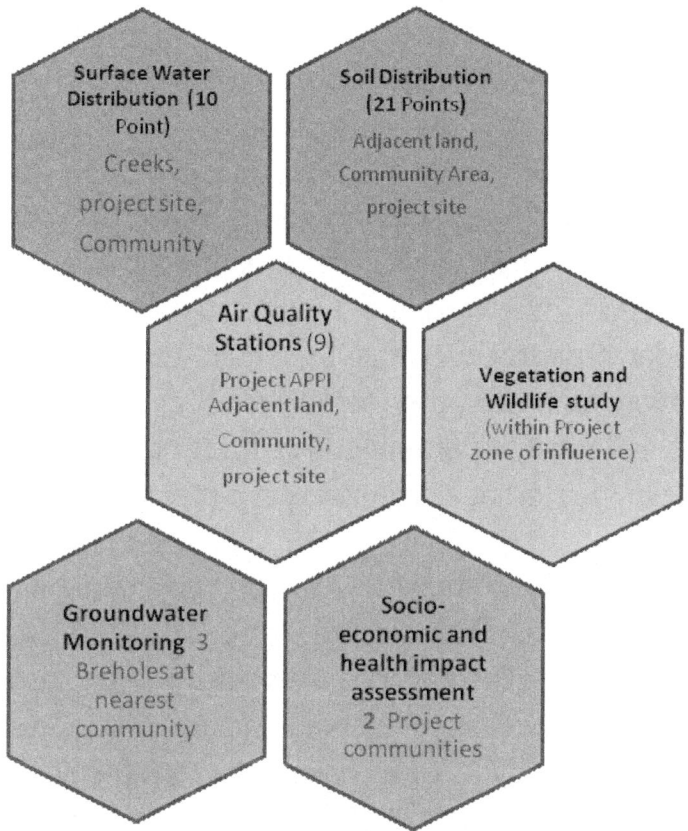

Fig 4.3: Illustration on sampling distribution

a) Logistics Plan, Meetings and Consultations

Great energies should be committed to putting in place sound logistics plan that will guarantee smooth implementation of the field data gathering exercise. Depending on the geographical location of the study area and distance from the base office of the proponent, plans are put in place for mobilization and the plan will involve coordination with the regulatory agencies, consultants and the project communities.

Plans for air travel, land transportation and water transportation as applicable must be consolidated prior to mobilization for field sampling. As a matter of fact if these plans are not firmed- up, field sampling exercise may be aborted.

While these plans are being firmed-up meetings, coordination and consultations with both internal and external stakeholders are activated. There must be internal alignment between the stakeholder departments within the organization, there must be coordination between the organization and the regulatory agencies and most importantly there must be consultation with the communities through community engagement efforts.

The essence is to obtain the support and cooperation of all interested parties that would likely clog the wheel of the field sampling exercise. For instance, there have been cases where community actions had prevented the EIA study team from accessing the study area because the community was not properly consulted and involved in the planning process.

a) Field Investigation Visit
Once activities in a-d above have been satisfactorily concluded, the EIA study team would be mobilized to the study area to implement the sampling plan in order to achieve the expectations of the EIA TOR/ SOW.

At the field, the sampling locations/ points as shown on the sampling map are established and corroborated by using Geographic Positioning System(GPS) equipment to establish the position to be sampled. Sampling in the field is guided by regulatory and best practices standards in order to collect appropriate samples and preserve the integrity of the samples collected. For example, soil samples are expected to be collected at top and bottom levels i.e. at 0-15cm (top) and 15-20cm (bottom) with the soil auger.

Composite sample (mixture of 3 successful grab samples) is to be collected for water sediment.

The field sampling pictures shown below are presented to reinforce the discussions presented above:

Fig 4.4: Soil sampling with Soil Auger

Fig 4.5: Soil Coring with corer.

Fig 4.6 : Sediment sampling with hand held grab

Fig 4.7: Grab deployment for seabed sampling.

Fig 4.8: Groundwater sampling from monitoring borehole

Fig 4.9: Sediment sampling and Benthos seiving

Fig 4.10: Carousel deployment for seawater profiling

Sample preservation and in-situ analysis

Because the different environmental samples have different physico-chemical properties and are affected differently by the environmental conditions such as temperature, light, humidity, atmospheric gases etc., there are guidelines and recommendations on how they should be collected, handled, preserved and stored in order to prevent contamination and deterioration of their qualities.

The table below adopted from Part VIII D, Table VIII – D of the DPR EGASPIN (2002) is instructive to guide.

S/N	Parameter	Required Volume (ML)	Container	Preservation	Maximum Holding Period
1	pH	35	Plastic,Glasss	Cool 4°C Determine on site	6 Hours
2	Electrical Conductivity	100	Plastic,Glasss	Cool, 4°C	24 Hours
3	Colour	50	Plastic,Glasss	Cool, 4°C	24 Hours
4	Odour	200	Plastic,Glasss	Cool, 4°C	24 Hours
5	Turbidity	100	Plastic,Glasss	Cool, 4°C	7 Days
6	Total Dissolved Solid (TDS)	50	Plastic,Glasss	Filter on site cool 4°C	24 Hours
7	Total Suspended Solid (TSS)	50	-	Filter on site	6 Months
8	Total Hardness	100	Plastic,Glasss	Cool,4°C HNO_3 to pH < 2	7 Days
9	Acidity and Alkalinity	100	Plastic,Glasss	Cool, 4°C	24 Hours
10	Salinity as Cl	50	Plastic,Glasss	None required	7 Days
11	Chemical Oxygen Demand (COD)	50	Plastic,Glasss	2ml H_2SO_4 per litre	7 Days
12	Biochemical Oxygen Demand (BOD)	1,000	Plastic,Glasss	Refrigeration at 4°C	6 Hours
13	Surfactant as (MBAS)	250	Plastic,Glasss	Cool,4°C	24 Hours
14	Dissolved Oxygen (DO)	300	Glass only	Determine On site	No holding
15	Ammonia	400	Plastic,Glasss	Cool, 4°C H_2SO_4 to pH < 2	24 hours
16	Oil & Grease	1,000	Glass only	Cool,4°C H_2SO_4 or HCL to pH < 2	24 Hours
17	Nitrate NO_3	100	Plastic,Glasss	Cool,4°C H_2SO_4 to pH <2	24 Hours
18	Sulphate $SO_2/4$	50	Plastic,Glasss	Cool,4oC	7 Days
19	Carbonate (CO_3) free CO & HCO_3	-	Plastic,Glasss	-	-
20	Cyanides	500	Plastic,Glasss	Cool 4°C NaOH to pH 12	24 Hours
21	Phosphorous	-	-	40 mg,$HgCl_2$ per litre 4°C	7 Days
22	Phenolic	500	Glass only	Cool,4°c H_2PO_4 to pH < 4	24 Hours
23	Chromium	100	Plastic,Glasss	HNO_3 to pH<2	-
24	Arsenic	100	Plastic,Glasss	HNO_3 to PH<2	6 Months

Table 4.1 : Choice preservatives and holding time for different parameters: Source (DPR EGASPIN, 2002)

As shown in the table above, some physico-chemical parameters are measured in-situ (on-site as they are being collected) because they have short retention period that if not measured as soon as they are collected, their values could be influenced by external physical environmental conditions thus presenting inaccurate and invalid results. Some of the parameters with which in-situ measurement are performed include:

- Temperature
- Dissolved oxygen
- pH
- TDS
- Conductivity etc.

4.4   Chain of Custody Procedures

The process of ensuring sample integrity from collection to analysis is known as chain of custody. This process includes the ability to track possession and handling of the sample from the time of collection through analysis and final disposition. This process is useful for routine control of samples integrity

Below are major aspects of chain of custody:

a.   Sample labels / tag: The sampling bottles/containers are labeled according to the respective type of samples. Labels are used to prevent sample misidentification. It is recommended that waterproof and oil-proof ink be used to label/tag the samples. The following information are included on the sample label or tag:

- Sampling date and time
- Sample identification

- Temperature
- Type of analyses required
- Name of sampler

b.   Field log book/Tracking Sheet: Sampling materials sent out are recorded on the tracking sheet to indicate the respective destinations, the date of dispatch, and what was dispatched. E-mails are also sent out by the field personnel to the base office for tracking purpose

c.   Sample Transportation: Samples collected in the field may be transported in batches if large samples are collected or moved to consultant laboratory as the field personnel demobilizes, whatever the scenario, the philosophy of sample transportation is that adequate measures are in place to prevent loss of liquid and vapour even the samples during transportation through the appropriate means of transportation such as by air, water or land in the appropriate secondary packaging as required by regulations for shipment. Before transportation to the lab, field personnel should check that the stopper provides a good seal to the sample container. This is to prevent loss of liquid and vapors during shipment. It also protects against moisture and dust.

4.5   Socio-economic data gathering

During field investigation, survey research is also conducted on the socio-economic component of the environment in order to understand the socio-cultural and economic characteristics of the people and their expectations/ concerns on the proposed project/activity.

The two survey research methodologies that are often used in conducting the socio-economic and health impact assessment are the Questionnaire administration and Interview preferably administered using the focus group discussion approach to collect data on socio-economic attributes and expectations of the people on the proposed activity.

On a general note the under listed actions are required to ensure QA/ QC of the samples collected

1) Clean field sampling techniques should be used to avoid contamination of samples.
2) Parameters with short or no-holding analytical time should be analyzed in-situ.
3) Separate samples should be collected for parameters requiring different treatment preservation before analysis.
4) Samples should be adequately preserved with recommended chemicals and properly labeled with water resistant markers.
5) Chain of custody form should be used for registration and tracking of sample from the field to the laboratory.

4.6   Laboratory and Data Analysis

The analysis of the physical, chemical and biological parameters of the environmental components as indicated in the EIA TOR/

SOW are carried out in accredited analytical laboratories and are based on standard methodologies and regulatory requirement as specified in Appendix VIII-D1 of the DPR EGASPIN (2002).

For instance, soil samples are analyzed for heavy metals (Fe, Zn, Hg, V, Ni, Ba, Pb, Cr, Cd, Cu, As),Oil and Grease, Total petroleum Hydrocarbon (TPH), Poly Aromatic Hydrocarbons (PAHs), Benzene, Toluene, Xylene and Ethelene (BTEX) Exchangeable cations (Na^{+}, Ca^{2+}, K^{+}, and Mg^{2+}), Anions (Cl^{-}, So_4^{2-}, No_3^{-} and Co_3^{2-} pH, Redox potential, Particle size, Organic content, Soil microbiology etc depending on the anticipated releases from project activities to establish the physic-chemical and biological properties of the soil in its current state.

The water samples may be analyzed for Physico Chemical such as pH, Dissolved Oxygen (DO), Total Suspended Solids (TSS), Total Dissolved Solids (TDS), Biological Oxygen Demand (BOD) Chemical Oxygen Demand (COD), plankton, in addition to the parameters listed above among others.

Other environmental components are analyzed for relevant parameters that would provide clue on the current physic-chemical characteristics of that component e.g. zooplankton and phytoplankton samples may be analyzed for species diversity and productivity etc. Benthic fauna samples may be analyzed for species abundance and distribution; vegetation samples may be analyzed to determine the existence of petroleum hydrocarbon in the tissue cell, presence of fungi and other microbes on the leaf foliage etc.

All environmental samples have standard procedures for their handling and analyses in the laboratory, and there are procedures for ensuring the validity and accuracy of the data through application of standard quality assurance/ quality control (QA/ QC) practices.

One key QA/ QC strategy is the use of blank and spiked samples and prevention of contamination and deterioration of sample; equipment duly calibrated and analysis done by experience personnel.

Laboratory analyses are expected to be carried out within the holding time of the respective parameter and only functional and

Fig 4.11: Laboratory analysis of samples

The socio-economic data are subjected to statistical analysis to provide the needed justification for conclusion made about the findings. Often times, large raw data are obtained from the field survey.

There are wide range of statistical techniques and tools for accomplishing the tasks of data analysis, the choice of statistical technique to which data will be subjected depends on the type of research design adopted and the kind of data obtained from the measurement scales (nominal, ordinal, ratio and interval).

Research in EIA study will fall into any or combination of research methods, historical research, descriptive research, correlation research, causal-cooperative research.

Depending on the magnitude of sample size and number of variables involved, quite enormous data may be generated and presenting them in the raw form may be cumbersome and difficult to understand and interpreted, hence the need for summary or organization of some sort in order to have a meaningful representation of the raw data. In this regard, descriptive statistics becomes useful in that it permits the description of very large data with relatively small number of indices. The category of study of statistics that is, a collection of methods used for organizing, classifying and summarizing numerical data is referred to as descriptive statistics.

Some of the commonly used statistics for describing raw data collected samples in EIA studies include frequency distribution, dispersion, relative position and relationship (correlation and regression).

The computer system is also commonly used for statistical analysis of research results. Commonly used statistical packages are Microsoft Excel for data analysis, statistical package for social sciences (SPSS) and STATISTICA.

Data on the socio-economic variables of the project communities would be analyzed and presented using the appropriate statistical method as discussed above.

4.7 Data Interpretation

When samples collected are analyzed, results are obtained, these results provide the basis on which inferences will be made and conclusions submitted on the findings. The generalizations that are made about the population from where samples used for the EIA study had been drawn are based on the results of analysis and their interpretations.

This aspect of the EIA study is very vital; this is because the validity, accuracy and reliability of the EIA report depend largely on the inferences drawn from the interpretation of both the physical and socio-economic environmental data.

In characterizing the project environment, correct and accurate interpretation of the results obtained from the analysis of the environmental parameters of the different environmental components is the underlying factor that determines the reliability of that description and impact predictions.

This explains why a team of multi-disciplinary experts should work together in providing specific expertise in the different areas of knowledge in the EIA study. For example an analytical chemist should be able to interpret the result of analysis of the physico-chemical parameters of environmental samples, where values are above threshold limit and deviate from what is obtainable in literature as standard values, explanation should be provided as to why the current value is as it is. For instance, if the pH value of the soil sample is below 4.0 the analyst should explain the possible reason(s) for the acidity of the soil sample.

The following physico-chemical parameters of soil will be used to strengthen the discussion on the importance of correct and accurate interpretation of data.

4.7.1 Total Nitrogen

Nitrogen is a very important plant nutrient involved in plant growth and photosynthesis. The total Nitrogen of the soil gives an indication of the organic nitrogen present in the soil which under suitable and adequate condition is capable of undergoing mineralization and therefore available for plant use. A soil high in organic matter content will have high total nitrogen.

Nevertheless, mangrove soils have been described as deficient in available nitrogen because of their high Carbon-Nitrogen ratio (Anderson 1967).

So, an interpretation of a soil value with high or low TOC should go further to explain the reason for that value.

4.7.2 Available Phosphorous

Phosphorus is one of the three plant nutrients or macro-nutrients. The tie-up of phosphorus is greatly affected by the pH level; it is mostly available in plants within the pH range of about 6.0 to 7.0. As the pH falls below 6.0, increasing amount of phosphorus gets tied-up in insoluble compounds with iron, aluminium and manganese while pH above 7.0, it starts forming insoluble compounds with calcium and magnesium. Inadequate supply of phosphorus can have a significant detrimental effect on plant growth, a situation where the phosphorus level is low and the pH value is below or above the optimum range of 6-7, the analyst should explain the possible reasons traceable to the pH of the soil.

4.7.3 Sulphate

Sulphate (SO_4^{2-}) is the stable highly oxidized form of sulphur. It can be produced by the bacterial oxidation of reduced sulphur compounds. Sulphates are also natural components of sedimentary rocks like shale. Appreciable quantities of sulphates exist in salt/ blackish water that flood the coastal soil regularly.

So, a mangrove soil for instance is expected to have high level of sulphate, the analyst should provide explanation of his interpretation of sulphate values if high or low in a mangrove soil.

4.7.4 Iron

Plants need a certain amount of iron to grow and thrive. Iron levels aid the chemical process, which creates optimum performance in plants and trees. The level of iron in soil is important to prevent them from weakening or even dying.

Iron serves to help plants and trees with photosynthesis to produce chlorophyll and energy. Without iron, the plants are unable to properly use all of the nutrients needed for photosynthesis. The proper balance of iron enables plants to thrive, for instance, reduced fruit and flower production, stunted growth and toxic iron buildup are common problems for vegetation in high-iron level soil.

Areas that are predominantly saturated with water or contain low levels of zinc contain high-iron soils. Areas around water tables are susceptible to high iron levels.

Mangrove soils and wetlands are predominantly saturated with water and these areas are susceptible to high iron. Also, geographical areas rich in pyrite are susceptible to high iron as a result of pyrite oxidation. Pyrite will slowly oxidize in a moist environment, and release sulfuric acid and Iron that is formed during the process. Considering the properties and chemistry of mangrove soils, it is expected that the iron concentrations are high.

4.7.5 Texture

Texture refers to the size and proportion of mineral particles (sand, salt and clay). Texture dictates water-retention capacity and drainage properties. It also indicates the ability of soils to retain and absorb nutrient and fertility thus influencing its productivity and management and it generally varies with depth. Based on the textural classes of the soil as obtained in the analysis, the analyst should provide scientific information that could guide the judgment on impact assessment and prediction with respect to spillages, percolation and leachates. He will not just stop at indicating that the soil is loamy, sandy or sandy-loam, he should explain the reasons and the implications.

4.7.6 Exchangeable Cation (Bases)

The exchangeable bases (Na^+ and K^+, Ca^{2+}, Mn^{2+} and Mg^{2+}) are important nutrient compounds of soil and its fertility. High Na^+ and Mg^{2+} values are typically associated with soils that are regularly flooded with salt/brackish water so mangrove soil. For instance, is expected to have high values of exchangeable bases; if the values are low, the analyst should explain the reason why it is so.

4.7. 7 Heavy Metals

Heavy metals pollution may occur when heavy metal laden waste is discharged into the soil/water environment. When this occurs, plant and animal may absorb those toxic elements and store it in their tissue. This may find its way to human system through the food chain.

Metals occupy the bulk of the periodic table of elements. The most current periodic table contains 118 elements, of which 18 are non-metals, 10 are metalloids and 90 are metals. Out of the 90 metals, 35 metals are of concern to us because of occupational or residential exposure; 23 of these are described as the heavy metals [Horsefall, 2011].

The heavy metals include antimony, arsenic, bismuth, cadmium, cerium, chromium, cobalt, copper, gallium, gold, iron, lead, manganese, mercury, nickel, platinum, silver, tellurium, thallium, tin, uranium, vanadium, and zinc.

In small quantities, certain heavy metals are nutritionally essential for a healthy life. These elements, or some form of them, are commonly found naturally in foodstuffs, in fruits and vegetables, and in commercially available multivitamin products [Horsefall, 2011].

Some are used in diagnostic medical applications such as direct injection of gallium during radiological procedures, the use of lead as a radiation shield around x-ray equipment and the use of silver and mercury amalgam for tooth filling

Essential heavy metals also have normal physiological regulatory functions. Heavy metals are also common in industrial applications such as in the manufacture of pesticides, batteries, alloys, electroplated metal parts, textile dyes, steel, catalysis and so forth Essential heavy metals become toxic when their amount exceeds those required for correct nutrition.For some heavy metals, toxic levels can just be a little above the background concentrations naturally found in nature. Long-term exposure to heavy metals may result in slowly progressing physical, muscular, and neurological degenerative processes. Allergies are also common and repeated long-term contact with some metals or their compounds may even cause cancer and eventual death [IOSHIC, 1999].

The sources of heavy metals are diverse and specific to each element. Heavy metals may be released into the environment by industrial, domestic and transportation processes. When released into the environment, they are washed into the soil by rain, and are taken up by plants, which are eventually consumed by grazing animals.

Heavy metals may also enter a water body such as streams, lakes, rivers, boreholes and groundwater by industrial and domestic effluents as well as from acid rain.Such metals find their way into parts of the body such as liver, lung, gizzards, kidney, and brain tissue, thereby compromising human health.

In general, the major sources of heavy metals in our environment may include:
*   Oil and gas activities
*   Industrial emissions and domestic applications
*   solid waste combustion
*   Agricultural applications and
*   Transportation processes

Toxicological symptoms of some Heavy Metals in Humans Heavy metal toxicity can result in damaged or reduced mental and central nervous function, lower energy levels, and damage to blood composition, lungs, kidneys, liver, and other vital organs of the body. The toxicological Symptoms of Some Heavy Metals are presented in Table 4.2 below

Metal	Toxicological Symptoms
Aluminum	Degenerative muscular conditions, Alzheimer's disease, Parkinson's disease and cancer, senility, and presently dementia
Arsenic	breathing problems; death if exposed to high levels; decreased intelligence; known human carcinogen: lung and skin cancer; nausea, diarrhea, vomiting; peripheral nervous system problems, skin pigmentation, abdominal pain
Bismuth	Renal failure
Cadmium	kidney damage and hypertension and all forms of cancer in human
Chromium	acute renal failure, Pulmonary and lung cancer
Cobalt	Goiter
Copper	Blue vomitus, shortage of blood, irritation
Iron	Vomiting, hemorrhage, stomach ulcer, liver failure and death
Lead	Behavioral problems; high blood pressure, anemia; kidney damage; memory and learning difficulties; miscarriage, decreased sperm production; reduced IQ and aggressiveness
Manganese	Parkinson-like syndrome, respiratory problems and , neuropsychiatric disorder
Mercury	blindness and deafness; brain damage; digestive problems; kidney damage; lack of coordination; mental retardation, autism, Parkinson's disease, Eczema
Nickel	Dermatitis, Eczema, acute lung injury, reduced sperm count, headache
Silver	bone marrow suppression, pulmonary edema, blue-grey discoloration of skin, nails, mucosae
Thallium	Vomiting, diarrhea, pain, coma,
Zinc	vomiting, diarrhea, abdominal pain, anemia,

Table 4.2: Toxilogical Symptoms of some heavy metals
Source: Michael Horsefall (2011)

Given that metals occurs naturally in varying concentrations in soil, for example, Iron (Fe) is characteristically high in mangrove soils due to oxidation of pyrite. Pyrite is a very common mineral found in a wide variety of geological formations from sedimentary deposits to hydrothermal veins and as a constituent of metamorphic rocks so heavy metal values other than Iron (Fe) above threshold value should be explained whether due to natural processes or metal pollution

4.7.8 Total Petroleum Hydrocarbons

Hydrocarbons are classified as organic compounds that contain Hydrogen and Carbon only. They can be of petroleum or recent biogenic origin.

Petroleum hydrocarbons are important environmental pollutants in terrestrial and aquatic environment. Natural plants and animals' hydrocarbons are ubiquitous in both terrestrial and aquatic ecosystem as they have been found in plant waxes, marine bacteria, and in benthic and plankton algae.

So, an elevated level of Total Petroleum Hydrocarbon in soil sample may not be necessarily due to petroleum contamination, it could be from biogenic origin or combination of both. The analyst should go a step further beyond the values and provide concise interpretation of the result of the analysis.

4.7.9 pH

The pH of soil can have an effect on plants by influencing the availbility of macro and micro nutrients which are building blocks for sugars and proteins to plants, lower limit pH is 4.8 and upper is 9.5 for optimum plant growth. Values beyond this range should be explained by the analyst. For instance, mangrove soil are acidic and values could be less than 4.8, this is as a result of the oxidation of pyrite,pyrite will slowly oxidize in a moist environment, and release sulfuric acid that is formed during the process, so if values less than 4 is obtained in the analysis, the analyst should provide explanation on why it is so.

4.7.10 Soil/WaterMicrobiology

Bacteria are of great epidemical importance to man as they may result in diseases such as cholera, enteritis, food poisoning, diarrhea, typhoid fever, dysentery, and fatal septicemia in man. Coliform bacteria are often used as biological indicators of faecal contamination, this is because they form part of the normal bacteria flora of the intestinal tract of animals and human beings, so if the population of E. coli is high in a soil/medium sample, the analyst should explain the possible sources of the contamination e.g. the target value of coliform in portable water is 0-1 MPN values above this indicates faecalpollution of the media

Microorganisms isolated from soil samples are classified into bacteria and fungi species. The presence of a bacteria species provides an indication of the state of the environment. For instance, pseudomonas aeruginosa, an important bacteria species organism in crude oil degradation. Their presence provide clue on the existence of petroleum contamination and also provide an assurance that biodegradation of crude oil will be boosted should it occur at the area.

The value of hydrocarbon degrading bacteria when higher than the limit of 10% is an indication of hydrocarbon pollution.

4.7.11 Macrobenthic Invertebrate

The distribution, abundance and diversity of benthic organisms are influenced by a multiplicity of factors such as immediate substrate occupation, salinity, pH, DO, food supply, currents, waves, tides etc.

Several groups of macro-benthic fauna are of special interest to fisheries, parasitological and pollution monitoring studies and many molluses such as periwinkles and bivalves are economically important.

The structure and function of benthic communities reflect the condition of the biotic and abiotic environment; they indicate shifts in the water quality. Because of their limited mobility and fairly long life span and environmental sensitivity, macro-benthic fauna are now widely used as reliable bio-indicators on pollution and impact assessment studies.

The interpretation of their abundance distribution and diversity should provide information on the current state of the benthic environment.

Conclusion

In characterizing the environment, different but interrelated activities such as field data gathering, samples analyses, data interpretation etc are carried out in order to provide detailed description of the current environmental status of the project area quantitatively and qualitatively.

The value of the field data is enhanced by good interpretation that presents information on the linear and inverse relationship between the different environmental parameters and inferences on the sensitivity of the project environment and thus susceptibility of certain environmental attributes. The relationship between the different environmental components and parameters are presented in clear and concise terms, to provide a sound platform and basis for evaluating and assessing the potential and associated impacts of the project, with a view to proffering effective mitigation measures required to protect and preserve the quality of environment processes within and around the Area of Potential Project Influence (APPI).

Chapter Five

IMPACT EVALUATION
AND ASSESSMENT

*This Chapter presents the impact assessment methodologies
and easy to use guidance on project impact identification,
assessment and prediction towards understanding
the basic elements and steps used in identifying and
assessing project impacts that is realistic and verifiable.*

The assessment of the potential and associated environmental and social impact of an activity/project is the central objective of an EIA. The value of an environmental assessment report depends largely on the ability of the report to identify and present relevant and key impacts that the proposed project activities may generate.

According to the DPR EGASPIN (2002), an environmental impact assessment report should assess all actions that will result in a physical, chemical, biological, cultural, social etc. modification of the environment as a result of the new project/development.

According to the EIA Act 86 of 1992, EIA is a study to identify, predict, evaluate and communicate information about the potential impacts of the proposed project on the environment and to detail out the necessary mitigation measures prior to project implementation.

The importance of accurate evaluation and assessment of project impacts cannot be over emphasized, this is because mitigation measures are developed based on the impacts identified and it is upon these measures that the environmental management strategies are based. Impact findings are expected to influence decisions on sites selection, technology option, engineering design and project implementation plan.

Impact identification can be likened to medical diagnosis of diseases, when the judgment of the diagnosis is wrong; the prescription will be misleading and ineffective.

This illustration paints the picture of how sound evaluation and assessment of environmental impacts and risks of a given project/development is critical in determining the success of an EIA.

In order to provide a sound estimate or judgment effects for natural, socio-economic and human receptor, it is important that a multidisciplinary team of experts with deep insight on the interactions between the project activities and environmental receptors be involved and committed to following the systematic processes in identifying, evaluating and predicting the project impact.

5.1 Identification of environmental, Socio-economic Aspects and Impact

Environmental Aspects in ISO 14001:2004 is defined as element of an organization's activities or products or services that can interact with the environment while impact is defined as any change to the environment, whether adverse or beneficial, wholly or partially resulting from an organization's environmental aspects.

Environmental aspects are generated at the different project phases (Fabrication, mobilization, construction/installation, operation and decommissioning) and the identification of the aspects specific to each phase is key in determining potential changes to the environment as a result of the project aspects.

Example of Environmental Aspects includes emission to air (smoke, dust, odor, fumes, etc.), waste water discharge to water stream or land, waste discharge to land, use of material, energy and resources, noise generation, vibration, radiation etc while impacts would be air pollution, water pollution, land pollution, noise pollution, natural resources depletion, nuisance, ozone depletion, global warming etc

The relationship between Environmental Aspects and Environmental Impacts can be best described as "CAUSE" and "EFFECT". One "CAUSE" could have one or multiple "EFFECTS".

5.2   Objectives of impact identification and assessment
The primary objectives of impact identification and assessment include:
1)   Establish the type (positive/ negative) of associated/ potential impacts that may occur as a result of a project/ activity being undertaken.

2) Differentiate between the insignificant impacts (those that can be sustained by the natural systems) and the significant impacts (those that cannot be sustained by natural systems).

3) To develop amelioration/ mitigation measures to address the significant negative impacts and determine enhancement measures for the positive impacts.

The following sections will provide detailed information on the impact assessment processes and methodologies.

5.3 Impact Assessment Methodologies

The key to a successful EIA is the use of appropriate impact identification, assessment and prediction methodology.

A variety of methodologies for impact assessment have been developed, these methods serve several purposes among which is the provision of organized approaches for impact analysis, nevertheless, these methods differ in their approaches to evaluating environmental impacts. The question is what impact assessment method is best to apply to a given project?

There is no single impact assessment method that meets all the requirements, of different projects; this explains why various Impact Assessment guidelines and methodologies have been developed to date and new ones emerging. Canter (1996) corroborated this that there is no universal methodology which can be applied to all project types in all environmental settings. UNEP (1996) supports the need to use tools from existing methodologies that best suit the specific project situation.

Impact assessment methodologies can be classified into three principal methods

Checklists: Checklists are comprehensive lists of environmental effects and impact indicators designed to stimulate the analyst to think broadly about possible consequences of contemplated actions. This strength can also be a weakness, however, because it may lead the analyst to ignore factors that are not on the lists.

Matrices: Matrices typically employ a list of human actions in addition to a list of impact indicators. The two are related in a matrix which can be used to identify (to a limited extent) cause-and-effect relationships. Published guidelines may specify these relationships or may simply list the range of possible actions and characteristics in an open matrix, which is to be completed by the analyst.

Flow diagrams. Flow diagrams are sometimes used to identify action-effect- impact relationships. The connections between a particular environmental impact and project action is established. e.g decrease in growth rate and size of commercial shellfish and coastal urban development as a result of dredging. The flow diagram permits the analyst to visualize the connection between action and impact. The method is best suited to single-project assessments, and is not recommended for large regional actions.

Though, there exist a number of methods and there is no specific regulation that mandates the use of a particular method, the

Scientific Committee On the Problems of the Environment (SCOPE) 1979 recommended some criteria which the chosen method should address:

1)   Is the method comprehensive?
2)   Is the method selective?
3)   Is the method mutually exclusive?
4)   Is the method objective?
5)   Does the method predict interactions?

The commonly used impact assessment methodologies fall under following types of approaches:

1)   The Leopold Matrix (Leopold et.al 1971)
2)   The tree diagram/Network analysis
3)   The Battle environmental evaluation system
4)   The overlay method
5)   Simulation Modeling
6)   ISO 14001process

5.3.1 The Leopold Matrix

The pioneering approach to impact assessment, the Leopold matrix, was developed by Dr. Luna Leopold of the United States Geological Survey (Leopold et. al., 1971). The matrix was designed for the assessment of impacts associated with almost any type of construction project. Its main strength is as a checklist that incorporates qualitative information on cause-and-effect relationships but it is also useful for communicating results.

The matrix involves the use of matrix with 100 specified actions and 88 environmental items to establish interactions between the actions and the environmental items. In the use of the Leopold matrix, each action and its potential for creating an impact on the environmental item must be considered. If an impact is anticipated a diagonal line is used to represent the point of intersection between the action and the environmental item.

The project actions and environmental characteristics are categorized in Part 1 and 2 shown below:

PART 1: Project Actions arranged horizontally on the matrix

A. MODIFICATION OF REGIME
a) Exotic flora or fauna introduction
b) Biological Controls
c) Modification of habitat
d) Alteration of ground cover
e) Alteration of ground-water hydrology
f) Alteration of drainage
g) River control and flow codification
h) Canalization
i) Irrigation
j) Weather modification
k) Burning
l) Surface or paving
m) Noise and vibration

B. LAND TRANSFORMATION
AND CONSTRUCTION
a) Urbanization
b) Industrial sites and buildings
c) Airports
d) Highways and bridges
e) Roads and trails
f) Railroads
g) Cables and lifts

E. LAND ALTERATION
a) Erosion control and terracing
b) Mine sealing and waste control
c) Strip mining rehabilitation
d) Landscaping
e) Harbour dredging
f) Marsh fill and drainage

F. RESOURCE RENEWAL
a) Reforestation
b) Wildlife stocking and management
c) Ground-water recharge
d) Fertilization application
e) Waste recycling

G. CHANGES IN TRAFFIC
a) Railway
b) Automobile
c) Trucking
d) Shipping
e) Aircraft
f) River and Canal traffic
g) Pleasure boating
h) Trails

h) Transmission lines, pipelines and corridors
i) Barriers, including fencing
j) Channel dredging and straightening
k) Channel revetments
l) Canals
m) Dams and impoundments
n) Piers, seawalls, marinas, & sea terminals
o) Offshore structures
p) Recreational structures
q) Blasting and drilling
r) Cut and fill
s) Tunnels and underground structures

C. RESOURCE EXRACTTION
a) Blasting and drilling
b) Surface excavation
c) Sub-surface excavation and retorting
d) Well drilling and fluid removal
e) Dredging
f) Clear cutting and other lumbering
g) Commercial fishing and hunting

D. PROCESSING
a) Farming
b) Ranching and grazing
c) Feed lots
d) Dairying
e) Energy generation
f) Mineral processing
g) Metallurgical industry
h) Chemical industry
i) Textile industry
j) Automobile and aircraft
k) Oil refining
l) Food
m) Lumbering
n) Pulp and paper
o) Product storage

i) Cables and lifts
j) Communication
k) Pipeline

H. WASTE EMPLACEMENT AND TREATMENT
a) Ocean dumping
b) Landfill
c) Emplacement of tailings, spoil and overburden
d) Underground storage
e) Junk disposal
f) Oil-well flooding
g) Deep-well emplacement
h) Cooling-water discharge
i) Municipal waste discharge including spray irrigation
j) Liquid effluent discharge
k) Stabilization and oxidation ponds
l) Septic tanks, commercial &. domestic
m) Stack and exhaust emission
n) Spent lubricants

I. CHEMICAL TREATMENT
a) Fertilization
b) Chemical deicing of highways, etc.
c) Chemical stabilization of soil
d) Weed control
e) Insect control (pesticides)

J. ACCIDENTS
a) Explosions
b) Spills and leaks
c) Operational failure

OTHERS

PART 2: Environmental 'Characteristics' and 'Conditions' listed vertically

A. PHYSICAL AND CHEMICAL CHARACTERISTICS

1. *Earth*
a) Mineral resources
b) Construction material
c) Soils
d) Landform
e) Force fields & background radiation
f) Unique physical features
2. *Water*
1) Surface
b) Ocean
c) Underground
d) Quality
e) Temperature
g) Snow, Ice, & permafrost

3. *Atmosphere*
a) Quality (gases, particulates)
b) Climate (micro, macro)
c) Temperature
4. *Processes*
a) Floods
b) Erosion
c) Deposition (sedimentation, precipitation)
d) Solution
e) Sorption (ion exchange, complexing)
f) Compaction and settling
g) Stability (slides, slumps)
h) Stress-strain (earthquake)
f) Recharge
i) Air movements

B. BIOLOGICAL CONDITIONS

1. Flora
1) Trees
b) Shrubs
c) Grass
d) Crops
e) Microflora
f) Aquatic plants
g) Endangered species
h) Barriers
I) Corridors

2. Fauna
a) Birds
b) Land anirnals including reptiles
c) Fish & shellfish
d) Benthic organisms
e) Insects
f) Microfauna
g) Endangered species
h) Barriers
I) Corridors

C. CULTURAL FACTORS

1. Land use
a) Wildemess& open spaces
b) Wetlands
c) Forestry
d) Grazing

d) Landscape design
e) Unique physical features
f) Parks & reserves
g) Monuments
h) Rare & unique species or

e) Agriculture
f) Residential
g) Commercia
h) Industrial
i) Mining & quarrying

2.*Recreation*
a) Hunting
b) Fishing
c) Boating
d) Swimming
e) Camping & hiking
f) Picnicing
g) Resorts

3. *Aesthetics & Human Interest*
a) Scenic views and vistas
b) Wilderness qualities
c) Open space qualities

ecosystems
i) Historical or archaeological sites
and objects
j) Presence of misfits

4. *Cultural Status*
a) Cultural patterns (life style)
b) Health and safety
c) Employment
d) Population density

5. *Man-Made Facilities and Activities*
a) Structures
b) Transportation network
(movement, access)
c) Utility networks
d) Waste disposal
e) Barriers
f) Corridors

D. ECOLOGICAL RELATIONSHIPS
SUCH AS:

1) Salinization of water resources
b) Eutrophication
c) Disease-insect vectors
d) Food chains
OTHERS

e) Salinization of surficial material
f) Bush encroachment

Instruction for Using the Leopold Matrix

In using the Leopold matrix to assess the impact of a proposed project, all the project associated activities are identified and placed on the horizontal axis (x- axis) while the environmental conditions are placed on the vertical axis (y-axis) and values are assign at the point of intersections to determine the magnitude and importance shown by a scale of 1-10 with 10 representing a very important interaction and 1interaction of relatively low importance.

The following instructions are to be embraced when using the Leopold Matrix

1) Identify all actions that are part of the proposed project.

2) Under each of the proposed action, place a slash at the intersection with each environmental item on the side of the magnitude if an impact is possible.

3) Having completed the matrix in the upper left hand corner of each box with a slash, place a number from 1 to 10 which indicates the MAGNITUDE of impact and 1 the least (No zeros). Before each number, place + if the impact would be beneficial. In the lower right hand corner of the box, place a number 1 to 10 which indicates the IMPORTANCE of the possible impact, 10 represents the greatest importance and 1 the least (No zeros).

4) The text which accompanies the matrix should be a discussion of the significant impacts, those columns and rows with large numbers of boxes marked and individual boxes with the large numbers.

Environmental Items	Project Activities					
	a	b	C	d	e	f
a		4/3		5/2	4/2	5/2
b	5/4	4/3	2/1	4/3	5/4	2/1
c		5/4	5/3			
d	3/2	4/2		5/4		5/3
e	2/1		3/2		4/3	
f	5/2	4/2	4/2	4/2		4/2
g	5/3	5/3	4/3	5/4		5/3
h	2/1		5/3	5/3	5/2	5/3

Table 5.1: Sample Matrix

NOTE: Assignment of important numerical value depends on the subjective judgment of the environmental assessment team. However, the matrix is a useful visual aid and fast cross reference for weight and values of information.

The matrix indicates that relationship between a project action and an environmental impact exists, but it does not indicate the nature or extent of the relationship neither can it be used to predict impact that would be generated.

The Leopold matrix is very useful as a gross screening technique for impact identification purposes and also effective in communicating results by providing a visual display on a single diagram.

The Leopold matrix is a flexible method of impact assessment which can be varied or modified to suit the type and scope of the project.

The modified Leopold matrix is commonly used in impact identification and assessment

The section below discusses other impact assessment procedures and the use of the modified Leopold matrix.

5.3.2 Scaling Weighting Techniques

Another example of the cross impact technique is what is known as the scaling-weighting techniques designed to remedy the short coming of the matrix approach. Under this technique, we have:

    a.   Tree diagram/network analysis

    b.   The battle environmental evaluation system

5.3.2.1The Tree Diagram/Network Analysis

The tree diagram involves the application of network analysis to environmental impact assessment. This method expands the concept of a matrix by introducing a cause condition effect network. This allows identification of cumulative or indirect or secondary effect not adequately explained through simple cause effect sequence represented by matrix. The network approach is useful in identifying various interrelationships between the casual factors of the project activities. It attempts to explicitly identify second and higher order impact by using variations of tree diagram to indicate the flow of impact through the environmental system.

The objective is not to show the impact directly resulting from project action as in matrix but to show the path of the primary impact through other paths of the system.

Impact trees can be a simple series of successive relationships in a chain or may form a branching tree of impacts.

Fig5.1 :Simple Series Impact Chain (Linear chain)

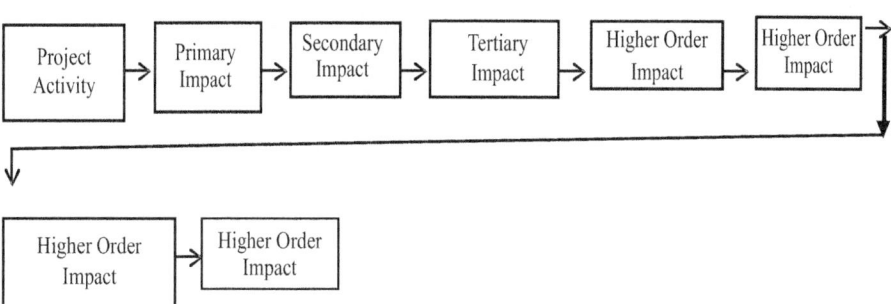

Branching tree of Impact

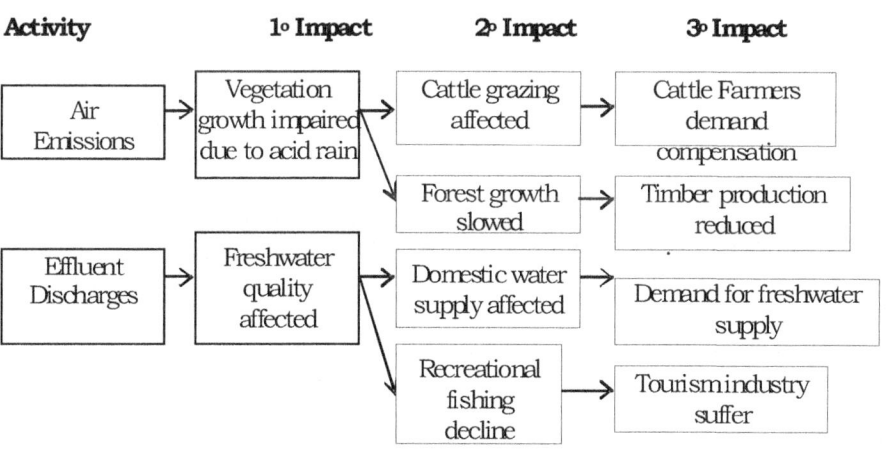

Fig 5.2: A network analysis of air pollution and effluent discharges.

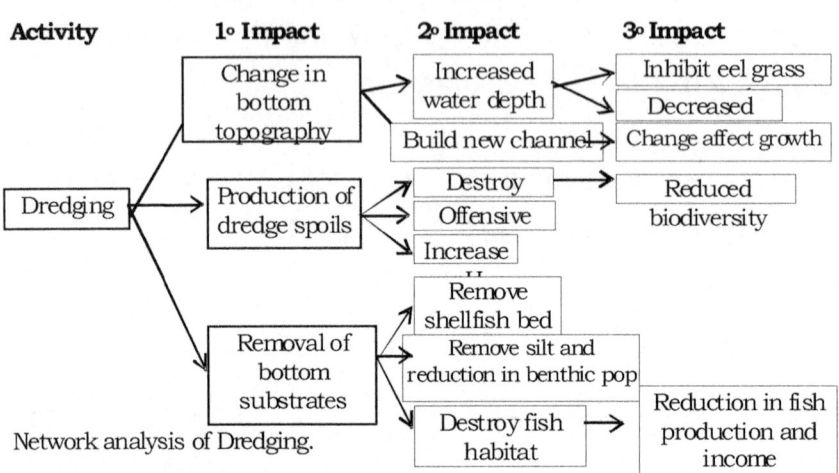

Network analysis of Dredging.

Actually the chain of impact is complex, it continues to lead to one another, the effect of the impact becomes more dispersed as it moves on.

The network analysis technique is very useful in predicting the higher order of impact that could be generated from the primary impact. It attempts to solve the problems of identifying higher order impacts.

For instance the impact of oil spill is not just a problem in a the immediate aftermath of a spill, when coastlines and wildlife are covered with oil slick. It wreaks a subtle, long-term havoc, as toxic chemicals enter ecological cycles and take decades to break down resulting in multidimensional impact conditions.

5.3.2.2 The Battele Environmental Evaluation System
Was developed by Battelle Columbus Laboratories in the USA to assess impacts of water resources development, water quality

management plans, highways, nuclear power plants and other projects (Dee et al 1972). The technique uses scaling-weighing checklist method which consists of a description of the environmental factors as well as instructions for listing all the parameters involved and assigning numbers to them according to their significance as judged by the team of experts.

The environmental parameters are organized into four sections such as:
1)   Ecology
2)   Environmental pollution
3)   Aesthetics
4)   Human interest.

These four human concerns are detailed in the table shown below:

Table 5.2 The Battelle Environmental Classification for Water-Resource Development Projects (Dee et al., 1973a). The Bracketed Numbers are Relative Weights

ECOLOGY

Terrestrial Species & Populations
-Browsers and grazers (14)
-Crops (14)
-Natural vegetation (14)
-Pest species (14)
-Upland game birds (14)

Aquatic Species & Populations
-Commercial fisheries (14)
-Natural vegetation (14)
-Pest species (14)
-Sport fish (14)
-Water fowl (14)

PHYSICAL/CHEMICAL

Water Quality
-Basin hydrologic loss (20)
-Biochemical oxygen demand (25)
-Dissolved oxygen (31)
-Fecal coliforms (18)
-Inorganic carbon (22)
-Inorganic nitrogen (25)
-Inorganic phosphate (28)
-Pesticides (16)
-pH (18)
-Streamflow variation (28)
-Temperature (28)
-Total dissolved solids (25)
-Toxic substances (14)
-Turbidity (20)

Terrestrial Habitats & Communities
-Food web index (12)
-Land use (12)
-Rare & endangered species (12)
-Species diversity (14)

Aquatic Habitats & Communities
-Food web index (12)
-Rare & endangered species (12)
-River characteristics (12)
-Species diversity (14)
Ecosystems

AESTHETICS
Land
-Geologic surface material (6)
-Relief & topographic character (16)
-Width and alignment (10)

Air
-Odour and visual (3)
-Sounds (2)

Water
-Appearance of water (10)
-Land & water interface (16)
-Odour and floating material (6)
-Water surface area (10)
-Wooded and geologic shoreline (10)

Biota
-Animals -domestic (5)
-Animals -wild (5)
-Diversity of vegetation types (9)
-Variety within vegetation types (5)

Man-Made Objects
-Man made objects (10)

Composition
-Composite effect (15)
-Unique composition (15)

Air Quality
-Carbon monoxide (5)
-Hydrocarbons (5)
-Nitrogen oxides (1
-Particulate matter (12)
-Photochemical oxidants (5)
-Sulphur oxides (10)
-Other (5)

Land Pollution
-Land use (14)
-Soil erosion (14)
Noise Pollution
-Noise (4

HUMAN INTEREST /SOCIAL
Education/Scientific
-Archeological (13)
-Ecological (13)
-Geological (11)
-Hydrological (11)

Historical
-Architecture and styles (11)
-Events (11)
-Persons (11)
-Religions and cultures (11)
-'Western Frontier' (11)

Cultures
-Indians (14)
-Other ethnic groups (7)
-Religious groups (7)

Mood/ Atmosphere
-Awe/inspiration (11)
-Isolation/solitude (11)
- Mystery (4)
-'Oneness' with nature (11)

Life Patterns
-Employment opportunities (13)
-Housing (13)
-Social interactions (11)

Each category contains a number of components that have been selected specifically for use in all U.S. Bureau of Reclamation water-resource development project.

For each component, Battelle has developed an index of environmental quality, normalized to a scale ranging from 0 to 1, using a value function method. Each impact indicator is then given as the difference in environmental quality between the states with and without action

The Battelle approach is mainly used by the U.S Bureau of Reclamation Water Resources but can be adapted for use in impact assessment.

The approach is comprehensive and at the same time selective on impact identification.

The numerical weighting scheme is explicit, permitting calculation of a project impact for each alternative. Although any type of weighting scheme is controversial, this one has been developed from systematic studies and its rationale documented.

5.3.3 The Overlay Technique

The overlay technique is a well defined approach used by geographers in town planning and landscape architecture. The technique was first suggested by Dr. LanMcharg (1968) and has since been widely applied in selecting alternatives and identify impacts.

The process of the overlay technique starts by subdividing the study/project area into convenient geographical units. Based on each of these geographical units and topographical features, the environmentalist collects information on the environmental factors and human concerns in the area through any or combination of the following methods; aerial photography, field observation, focus group discussions and questionnaire.

The concerns are arranged into a set of factors each having a common basis e.g. land elevation, water bodies, vegetation, settlement etc. The physical space is usually divided into grid cells. In this grid cells, demographic information and various characteristics are represented graphically in transparent maps, these transparent overlays are then superimposed on one another when overlaid, and they help assist to locate the position of the project and giving the geographical scale of the project. They can give you the degree of concentration or dispersal of the project influence and impact.

Meanwhile this conventional method of generating overlays has been revolutionized by the powerful technology of remote sensing and Geographic Information System (GIS) as observed by FAO (1991), is a field of applied science and technology which has recently emerged that when used in combination can greatly assist in spatial decision-making process. The first is remote sensing technology which is supported by high resolution environmental satellites and sensing devices to capture geographic information which can be processed and applied to solve wide ranging and specific environmental problems. This task can be greatly expedited by using the second applied science and technology field, that of geographic information system (GIS) which relies on the increasing power of the computer to process vast amounts of information in such a way as to produce any desired maps, tabular or textual output using a large array of data to produce overlay maps. It is necessary to prepare maps that show the position, nature and extent of natural and human attributes of an area. Attributes which may be mapped include surface water bodies, agricultural lands, wetlands, settlement etc.

With high degree of accuracy, overlay maps can be produced, with GIS providing detailed information on many environmental variables covering a broad array of spectral, temporal and spatial scales.

The objectivity of the overlay method is high with respect to the spatial positioning of effects and impacts (e.g., area of land to be flooded), but is otherwise low. Overlays are not effective in estimating or displaying uncertainty.

Overlay approach is very useful in data description for environmental planning and project development. It is valuable in making an inventory of information on a large number of variables and in an illuminating complex spatial relation. For instance in the planning's of development of an engineered landfill, the overlay technique can be used in identifying existing roads, schools, residential areas, historic sites, water bodies, pipelines, agricultural areas, recreational areas, etc. and in analyzing such information spatially in the various geographical units. Because geographic data can be assessed, transformed and manipulated interactively, they served as test bed for studying environmental processes or for analyzing the trend of results of planning decision.

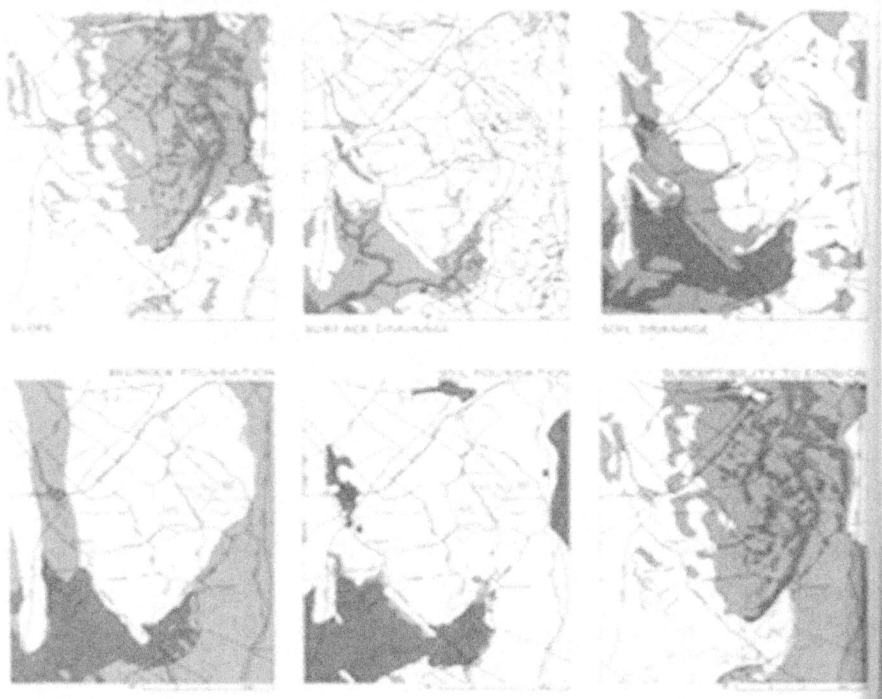

Figure 5.3: Overlay map adapted from Lan McHarg (1968)

Overlay map can be used to present large amount of spatial data to display information about the natural environment in a meaningful way.

In using the overlay technique, the various geographical entities can be classified under natural system, economic system and social system.

For each environmental factor and each geographical unit, an impact rating of 1 (Low) to 4 (High) can be assigned and a special number such as 5 will be sensitivity of the environmental and socio-economic receptors.

The overlay approach has the advantage of predicting spatial patterns. The capability of GIS spatial analysis tools can be used in conducting time-series/trend analysis which will provide clear information on the interrelationship between the project and the environmental settings now and in the future given that certain condition are fulfilled.

The method can be used to communicate clear and easily understood interactions of a given project with other environmental and socio-cultural components in an environmental setting.

5.3.4 Simulation Modeling

Model is designed to imitate in an approximate fashion the features of a complex system. It is potentially a sophisticated forecasting tool which expresses mathematically, relationships and interrelationships among influencing factors and events in an environmental system over time.

The potential advantages of a simulation model are great and hold future promise for impact assessment.

Computer models are used in the prediction of impact on the receiving environment. Computer models have been used for effluent discharge modeling, air dispersion modeling, oil spill modeling, drill cuttings modeling etc.

Models can be used to delineate vulnerable areas provide guide on impact quantum, aerial extent of impact, determines if releases/emission will significantly increase background levels beyond acceptable standards.

Models allow quantitative evaluation of impacts thereby making quantitative analysis and prediction possible.

Computer models are essential as additional tools used to complement other impact assessment methodologies particularly when a specialized impact study such as air emissions are to be conducted.

5.4   Major Steps for Impact Assessment

The major impact assessment steps using the modified Leopold Matrix is shown below:

Step 1: Identification and description of project phases associated activities and their possible interaction with environment, social and health component.

Step 2: Preliminary identification of potential impacts on environmental social and health components (using impact indicators indices).

Step 3: Screening of impact importance (Here activity environment interaction producing no effects are eliminated and focus impacts are selected for further assessment.

Step 4: Detailed assessment of selected focus impacts to determine:

      a.   Nature (positive or negative, direct or indirect)

      b.   Magnitude (qualitative and quantitative)

      c.   Area extent

      d.   Frequency

      e.   Duration

      f.   Sensitivity (resource sensitivity)

      g.   Serenity

      h.   Cumulative effort

Step 5: Final assessment and assignment of overall impact severity level (Impact significance level) based on step 4 results and application of consequence and likelihood criteria. This step can be represented as shown in the flow chart below:

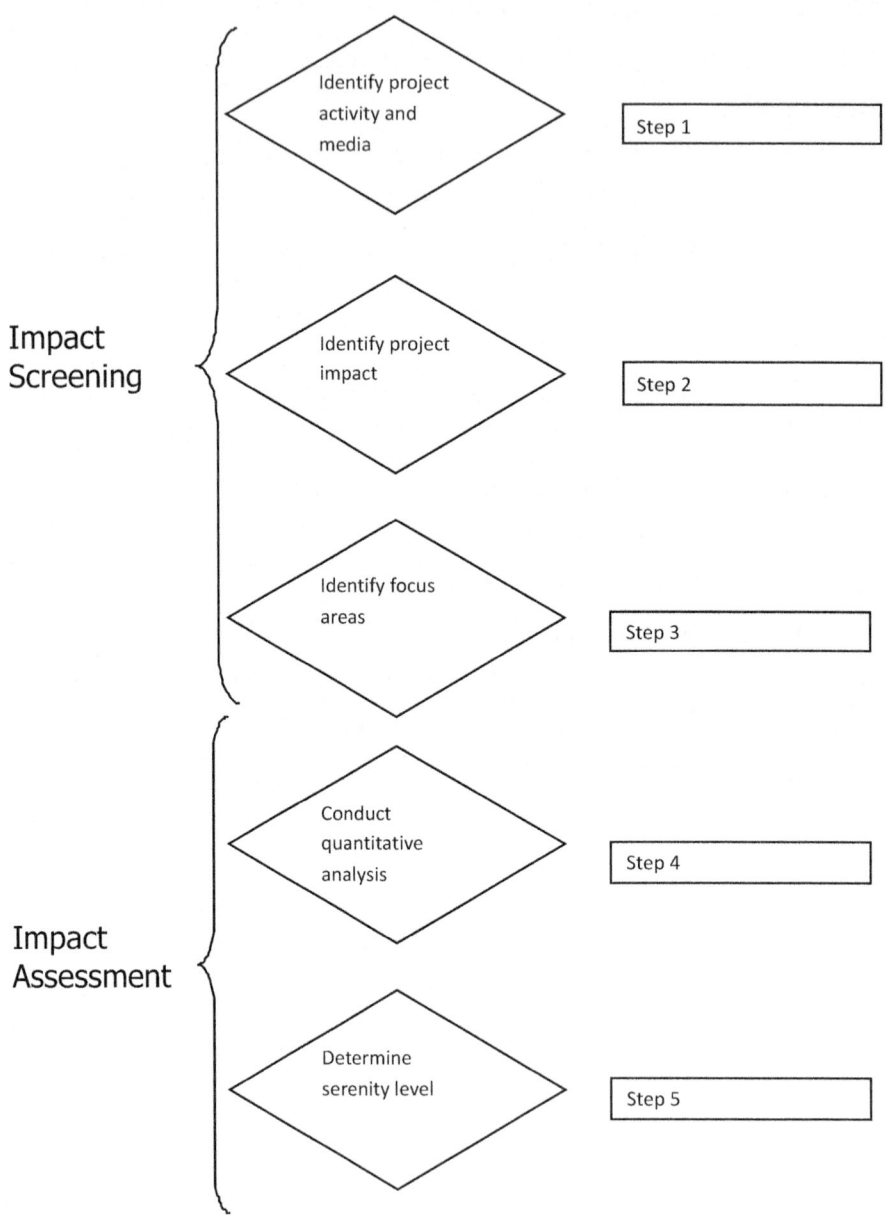

5.4.1. Step 1:Identification and description of project phases associated activities and their possible interaction with environment, social and health component

This step involves the identification and description of project phases and associated activities. For instance, project phases would involve mobilization/installation, commissioning, operation and decommissioning.

In each of these phases, details of the associated activities should be outlined, then the possible interactions of these activities with the environmental, social and health components.

The interaction can be determined by listing the project activity on the y-axis and the environmental, social and health components on the x-axis. Possible interaction is indicated at the point of intersection and the cell is marked to indicate interaction

Receptors / Project Activities	Physical	Biological	Socio-economic	Others
Site Preparation e.g: bush clearance, Road construction Dredging Piling etc	X	X	X	
Mobilization e.g movement of men and materials Supply vessel movement etc	X	X	X	X
Construction e.g installation of pipeline installation of prefabricated modules etc	X	X	X	
Commissioning e.g pre start up commissioning activities Start of beneficial operation			X	X
Operation When the project has fully transited to operations phase	X	X	X	X
Decommissioning e.g end of project life cycle decommissioning and abandonement	X	X	X	X

Table 5.3: Identification and description of project phases and associated activities.

Environmental Indicator groups — **AIR QUALITY:** Particulates, Gaseous Hydrocarbons, NOx·SOx · **WATER QUALITY:** Turbidity, Temperature, Chemical Parameters · **SEABED QUALITY:** Seabed Physico-chemistry, Beaches/shores · **AQUATIC ECOLOGY:** Plankton, Marine mammals/reptiles, Pelagic fishes, Benthic Flora & Fauna, Mangrove ecosystems

Project Activities	Particulates	Gaseous Hydrocarbons	NOx, SOx	Turbidity	Temperature	Chemical Parameters	Seabed Physico-chemistry	Beaches / shores	Plankton	Marine mammals / reptiles	Pelagic fishes	Benthic Flora & Fauna	Mangrove ecosystems
Pre-construction													
Mobilisation of construction element	×	×	×	×			×						
Construction & installation													
Pipeline installation: seabed works, anchoring.				×		×	×		×	×		×	
Pipeline installation wastes (end mills, flux, oils from machinery)	×			×		×	×		×	×	×	×	
Piling, utilities installation..	×			×		×	×		×	×	×	×	
Power Generation	×	×	×										
Effluent discharges					×	×	×		×	×	×	×	
Painting and coating	×					×		×	×	×	×		
Emissions from supply vessels movement	×	×	×		×			×	×	×	×		×
Support Logistics	×		×										
Construction waste handling						×	×		×	×	×	×	
Welding.	×												
Operation													
Mineral extraction and transportation		×			×	×						×	
Turbines / Essential Generators	×	×	×										
Open Drain System		×											
Wastes Handling (sewage, solid, sanitary, biodegradable)						×	×		×	×	×	×	
Maintenance activities		×	×										
Chemical Storage and usage						×	×	×	×				
Pumps and generator use	×	×	×										
Facility Maintenance Works	×												
Supply and Support Logistics	×		×										
Transportation of raw materials and finished goods		×				×	×	×	×	×	×	×	×
Pigging, cleaning, gauging and hydrostatic testings						×	×		×	×	×	×	×
Geo-hazards							×	×	×	×	×	×	
Public Concerns / Interference													
Decommissioning													
Accidental Fires / Blasts	×	×	×		×			×	×	×	×		×
Platform / LOP decommissioning	×		×	×			×		×	×			
Pipeline decommissioning	×		×	×			×		×	×	×	×	

Table 5.4: Typical Activities-Environment Interaction Matrix

5.4.2. Step 2: Project Impact Identification

Having established the possibility of interactions between project activities and the environmental components, the preliminary identification of potential impacts on environmental, social and health components using impact indicators indices is carried out. The table of impact indicators is as shown below.

Environmental components	Impact indicators
Biophysical/ Terrestrial	
Geology	Changes to geology, geomorphology, topography.
Soil	Changes to physical, chemical properties and soil ecology.
Vegetation	Changes to vegetation population, health, species abundance and diversity and impact on endangered and economic species.
Surface water	Changes to water quality indices, hydrocarbons metals and hydrobiology. Introduction of exotic species, destruction of habitats, abundance, diversity, endangered species.
Groundwater	Changes to water quality indices, hydrocarbon metals. Groundwater abrasion, changes to flow direction and subsidence.
Marine Ecology	
Fish and marine mammals	Changes in migratory pattern, food chain impact, fish and other fauna diversity and abundance, effect on juveniles and endangered species.
Marine water	Changes in productivity, plankton abundance and diversity. Changes to water quality indices.
Marine birds	Mortality, migratory patterns, food chain effects.
Sea bed	Change in diversity and abundance of benthic organism from physical and chemical impact.

Coastal habitat	Impact on sensitive coastal habitats endangered and protected species. Changes in fish and fauna diversity, abundance and effect on juvenile, nesting areas etc.
Air	Increase in concentrations of NO_x, SO_x, Pm, CO, Green house gases.
Noise and vibration	Increase in noise and vibration levels.
Aesthetics	Impairment of the quality of the physical environment.
Socio-economic	
Population	Changes in population indices, total population gender ratio, age distribution.
Infrastructure	Improvement or pressure on existing infrastructure including waste handling facilities.
Social and cultural structure	Impact to local authority and governance structure, increase in negative social vices e.g. prostitution, crime, intra and inter ethnic clashes.
Cultural and Archeological resources	Impact on shrines, burials grounds, loss of archeological resources.
Transportation	Increase in different types of transportation.
Health and Security	Impairment or improvement of health of workers and of general public, increased security risk.
Macro and micro economy	Improvement or negative impact on macro and micro economy, employment, standard of living, occupation changes.

Table 5.5: Impact indicators

Based on the knowledge of the associated activities of the proposed project, it is determined whether those activities would have potential impact on the environment, taking clues from impact indices relative to the environmental social and health components as a result of the project.

The determination of possible interaction between project activities and the environmental components and the identification of potential impacts are complementary exercise.

The essence is to be able to eliminate activity-environment interaction that is producing no effect so as to pay attention to activity-environment interaction that will generate impacts.

5.4.3. Step 3: Screening of Impact Importance
Activity in step 3 is still tied to the activities in step 1 and 2. As a matter of fact, step 1 to 3 activities represent impact identification stage.

The key action of step 3 is to identify activity-receptors producing effect and those producing no effect are eliminated and those producing effect are selected for further assessment.

5.4.4. Step 4: Detailed Impact assessment
This commences in step 4 whereby quantitative and qualitative assessment are conducted to determine:
    a.   Type – biophysical, social, health or economic
    b.   Nature of impact (positive or negative, direct or indirect).
    c.   Magnitude or severity (high, moderate, low)

d. Area extent (localized, regional or national or transboundry)
e. Frequency (time scale)
f. Duration (short, medium or long term)
g. Sensitivity (resource sensitivity)
h. Cumulative effect
i. Reversibility (reversible/irreversible)

Impact Duration can be defined in term of recovery period as

Short term = 0 - 6 months
Medium = 6 months – 1 year
Long term = > 1 year.

Based on the judgment derived from consideration of the above listed impact criteria, ranking of the potential impact are on a scale such as A- E, interpreted as follows:

A = Very low impact (insignificant)
B = Low impact (insignificant)
C = Moderate impact (significant)
D = High impact (significant)
E = Very high impact (significant)

In addition, positive (+) or negative (-) signs are used to indicate beneficial or adverse impacts.

Having defined these criteria, quantitative assessment of impact is carried out using the impact matrix. The Leopold matrix can be modified to carry out the impact assessment.

The table below shows the illustration of the use of modified Leopold matrix impact assessment of an onshore gas project.

Project Activities	Environmental components and impact receptors.										
	Physical				Biology			Socio-economic & Health			
Activities at different phase	Soil	Surface Water	G.Water	Air	Flora Diversity	Fauna Diversity	Veg	Cultural	Income	Arche	P.Health
Pre-constr		C-									
Mobilization		C-		C-				C+			
Site prep	C-						D-				
Construction											
Pipelaying/dredging			C-								
Process plant installation											
Operations								C+		B+	
Maintenance											
Waste mangt		C-	B-								
Decommissioning											

Table 5.6: Modified Leopold Matrix

The matrix above can be interpreted as follows:

Mobilization of personnel, equipment and materials would interact with the surface water to produce a negative but moderate impact denoted by (C-).

Site preparation exercise would interact with soil to produce moderate and negative impact (C-), negative and high impact will be produced by the interaction of site preparation activities with vegetation, and this is denoted by (D-) this is because a large area of vegetation cover will be cleared at the project site.

Basis for the Assessment

The decision on the scale on activity-receptor impact is ranked depending on the following:

1) Knowledge of the project activities, equipment types and layout of the facilities as provided in project and process description of section, process inputs and outputs including waste streams.
2) Results of the field sampling and laboratory analysis which provides the inferences on the sensitivity of the project environment and thus susceptibility of certain environmental attributes.
3) Legal/Regulatory requirements and expectations
4) Public perception and interest
5) Findings on the review of other reports on similar project/ environment.
6) Multidisciplinary experts' judgment based on professional experiences.

The Federal Ministry of Environmental EIA sectoral guidelines for oil and gas industry project provides some body of knowledge on what impact to expect from the different phases of oil and gas offshore project.

a. Impacts due to project location/siting:
    The impacts on the coastal and marine environment by exploration and production activities, offshore starts from the location of the exploration area. The impacts will be on the aquatic ecosystem, sediment physico-chemistry and biology, fisheries, oceanography etc.

The potential environmental impact linked with the location/siting of oil and gas development offshore which should be considered includes:
*   Conflict with native culture, traditions and areas lifestyles.
*   Obstruction of boat traffic by offshore facilities.
*   Interference with drainage pattern on-shore.
*   Disturbance of cultural resources, benthic communities, mangroves, coastal barriers, wetlands, pipelines and cables.
*   Disturbance of human and wild life by increased noise levels in coastal areas from aircraft over flights, ship traffic and facility operation.
*   Loss of beach areas to pipeline landfalls and support facilities.
*   Degradation of sea-ward vista (aesthetics).
*   Disturbance of marine mammals by sensitive surveys, drilling and shipping.
*   Loss or reduction of fishing area and recreation sites.

b. Impacts due to construction:

Construction related activities which include pile driving, material transportation, building of platform, dredging can produce significant environmental impacts. The key potential environmental impacts associated with construction that should be considered in the EIA report should include:

- Drainage of cultural and historical resources.
- Disturbance of ecosystems and environmentally sensitive areas (estuaries, mangrove, spawning ground etc.)
- Nuisance by noise, dust, fumes, fires, explosion.
- Flooding hazards due to construction.
- Air pollution by emissions from impediment to natural wave's patterns and actions.
- Blockage of fisheries migratory path.
- Disturbance of bottom sediments and benthic organisms.
- Impact on hydrological balance on-shore.

c. Impact relating to project operations:

- Degradation of coastal and offshore waters by discharges during routine operations (e.g. effluents, sanitary waters, production water and spills).
- Degradation of air quality from routine operational emissions (e.g. combustion, venting, spills).
- Air pollution from flaring, sour gas discharge and burning of oil waste and shidge pits.
- Mortality and /or reduced reproduction of marine

flora and fauna, sea birds and water fowl resulting from oil and chemical spill.

- Mortality and/or reduced reproduction of benthic organisms, coral communities and other marine life through smothering.
- Degradation of beach areas, coastal facilities and boat by oil spills and littering (e.g. coasting, tar balls, trash and debris from offshore and transport).
- Noise nuisance from equipment operations, truck traffic, helicopter over flight.
- Injury/loss of life from accidents in transportation and facility operation.
- Loss of beach areas due to pipeline, landfalls and support facilities (e.g. land use, impact of soil, clean up activities, use of dispersant, traffic, soil contamination).
- Loss of drilling rigs due to instability and characteristics of the sea floor.

The nature of interaction and impacts ranked will depend on the nature and scope of the project/action and the environmental setting where the project will be located, nevertheless, the basis of assessment outlined earlier and the characteristics impacts of oil and gas development project identified by the FME_{NV} EIA sectoral guideline are instructive to guide in the judgment of the quantitative and qualitative assessment of associated and potential impacts of a given project on the environment using the modified Leopold Matrix.

5.4.5. Step 5: Final assessment and assignment of overall impact severity levels.

Based on the result of the assessment in step 4, impact significant level is determined by the application of consequences and likelihood of the impact/risks. The significance level is mathematically expressed as the product of the consequence and likelihood.

So, impact significance = Consequence x Likelihood.

Definition of these two key elements:

1) Consequence: The resultant effect (positive or negative) of an activity's interaction with the biophysical), socio-economic and health environment.

2) Likelihood: The likelihood that an effect or impact resulting from specific project activity will occur.

To assign consequence and likelihood to an impact, a 5 x 5 or 6 x6 matrix with criteria well defined and ranked could be used.

CONSEQUENCE

5 categories of consequences can be ranked as follows:

Catastrophic = 5
Major   = 4
Moderate   = 3
Minor   = 2
Negligible   = 1

The criteria for consequence ranking is shown in table 5.7 a &b below. Table 5.7a Categories and definition of consequences levels for biophysical impacts:

Category	Ranking	Definition

Catastrophic (worst case scenario)	5	• Trans-boundary and/or national scale impact resulting in
		  - Long term and profound change and/or damage to the natural environment and its ecological processes
		  - Increase in threat for rare and endangered species of fauna and flora identified in natural and global listing.
		• Natural habitat restoration time greater than 10 years and requiring large-scale and long-term intervention.
		• Breach of environmental regulations and/or company policy and/or greater than 200% exceedance of international industry and/or operator standard for emission and effluent parameters.
		• Negative under spread natural and international media coverage.
		• Significant long-term financial loss.

Major	4	• Regional to national scale impact resulting in:
		  - Medium term change and/or damage to the natural environment and its ecological processes.
		  - Reduction in regional habitat and species diversity and/or direct loss of habitat for endemic, rare and endangered species of fauna and/or flora and for species' continued persistence and viability.
		• Natural habitat restoration time 5 to 10 years and requiring substantial intervention.
		• Breach of environmental regulations

Moderate	3	• Local to regional scale impact resulting in : - Short term change and/or damage to natural environment and its ecological processes. - Direct loss of habitat crucial for specie continued persistence and viability - Introduction of exotic species of fauna or invasive floral species replacing resident natural communities within the project area and - Environmentally stress lowering reproductive rates of species within the project area. • Natural restoration time ~ to 5 years and requiring intervention • Potential breach of environmental regulations and company policy and/or 50 to 100% exceedance of international, national, industry and/or operator standard for emission parameter. • Complaints from the public authorities and possible local media attention.
Minor	2	• Local scale impact resulting in : - Short term change and/or damage to local natural environment and its ecological processes. - Short term decrease in species diversity in selected biotopes/ areas within the project area and/or - Increased mortality of fauna species due to direct impact from project activities. • Natural restoration within 2 years requiring minimal or no intervention • 10 to 50% exceedance of international, national, industry

Negligible	1	• Impact largely not discernable on a local scale being absorbed by the natural environment, areas adjacent to disturbed areas • Restoration within 6 months without intervention. • Up to 10% exceedance of international, national, industry and/or operator standard for emission parameter. • Public perception/concern • Minimal financial loss.

Positive	+	• Activity has net positive and beneficial effect resulting in environmental improvement, for example:
		  - Ecosystem health
		  - Increase in magnitude or quality of habitat for rare and endangered species of fauna and flora as well as for those species known to naturally occur in the area.
		  - Growth of naturally occurring population of flora and fauna
		• Positive feedback from stakeholders.
		• Potential financial gain.

Table 5.7b: Categories and definition of consequence level for socio-economic and health impacts

Category	Ranking	Definition
Catastrophic	5	• Emergency situation with harmful consequences to human health • Disastrous consequences on the likelihoods of individuals (e.g. curtailment of access to primary income source) • Calamitous consequences on those seeking to access community facilities and utilities (e.g. resettlement of large number (1,000) of households). • Disastrous consequences on the national economy. • Breach of company social policy and/or legislation.

Major	4	• Major impacts on human health (e.g. serious injury) • Significant impact on the livelihood of individuals (i.e. access to income source restricted over lengthy period of time). • Serious impact on access to community facilities and utilities (e. g. resettlement of large numbers (10 – 100) of households). • Notable consequence on the economy at a local, regional and/or national level (e.g. virtually no local sourcing of supplies or personnel. • Breach of economy social policy and/or regulation.
Moderate	3	• Modest impact on human health and well being (e.g. noise, light, odor, dust, injuries to individuals. • Moderate impact on individual livelihoods (e.g. restricted access to

Minor	2	• Limited impact on human health and well-being (e.g. occasional dust, odor, traffic, noise) • Same impact on the livelihoods of individuals (e.g. isolated incidents related to ethnic tensions and some restrictions on access to income source). National restoration within 2 years requiring minimal or no intervention. • Same impact on access to community facilities and utilities (e.g. access to cultural centers restricted to a limited extent (i.e. days). • Sparse impact on the wider economy at a local, regional and national level (e.g. limited procurement).
Negligible	1	• Possible nuisance to human health and well being (e.g. occasional unpleasant odors). • Very limited disruption caused to those earning

Limited positive	+	<ul><li>Same beneficial improvement to human health.</li><li>Same benefits to individual livelihood, (e.g. additional employment opportunities).</li><li>Limited improvements to community facilities/utilities (e.g. no discernable improvement).</li><li>Same impact on the wider economy (e.g. limited local procurement).</li></ul>
Modest positive	++	<ul><li>Moderate beneficial improvement to human health.</li><li>Medium benefits to individual livelihoods (e.g. employment impact).</li><li>Modest improvements to community infrastructure/utilities.</li><li>Moderate impact on the wider economy (e.g. same local sourcing of supplies).</li></ul>
Significant positive	+++	<ul><li>Major beneficial improvement to human health.</li></ul>

LIKELIHOOD

Five categories of likelihood can be ranked as follows:

Certain/ very high	= 5
Occasionally/High	=4
Seldom/medium	= 3
Highly unlikely/low	= 2
Remote/very low	= 1

The criteria for likelihood are shown in table 5.8 below.

Table 5.8: Likelihood categories and rankings of natural and socio-economic impact.

Category		
Very high	5	Given controls in place, the impact will definitely occur during normal operations (i.e. 100% likelihood of occurring, impact has been known to result in all similar circumstances).
High	4	Given the controls in place, the impact is likely to occur during normal operations (e.g. over 70% likelihood of occurring, impact has been known to result routinely though not necessarily in all similar circumstances).
Medium	3	Impact could occur in frequently during normal operations but given a breakdown of safeguards and controls (i.e. lack of maintenance for a protecting dence). It could occur more readily (e.g. between 20 and 70% likelihood of occurring; impact has been known to result in many similar circumstances but does not result routinely).

Low	2	Impact highly unlikely, given the controls in place (e.g. between 2 and 20% likelihood of occurring, impacts has been known to result but only very rarely in similar circumstances).
Very low	1	Impact has less than 1 or 2% likelihood of occurring, impact unknown to have previously resulted in similar circumstances in the industry.

5.5 Impact Significance Severity

The impact severity level is mathematically expressed as the product of the consequence and likelihood i.e. Consequence x Likelihood = Severity.

To compute the potential impact of the project activities on the recipient environment i.e. determine the impact significance/severity, the modified Leopold interaction matrix based on consequence and likelihood of the impact is developed. Every identified aspect/interaction is assessed based on the definitions of consequence and likelihood categories and the product of these interactions determines the overall significance of the impact. For instance, if the consequence of an activity on the environment high (5) and the likelihood of occurrence is moderate (3), the overall impact significance ranking will be 15.

The value assigned to each cell in the matrix is in the form "x(y)" where x denotes the consequence and x, the likelihood of the impact.

The table 5.4 below provides an illustration of the assignment of values for the consequence and likelihood ranking in order to determine the impact significance of a given project on the environment

Project Activities	Environmental components and impact receptors.										
	Physical				Biological			Socio-economic & Health			
Activities at different phase	soil	Surface water	g.water	air	Flora diversity	Fauna diversity	veg	cultural	income	arche	P.Health
Pre-construction	3(2)										
Mobilization		4(2)		3(2)					+		
Site prep construction		3(3)									
Pipelaving/dredgin			3(2)								
Procees plant installation											
Operations									+		3(2)
Maintenance											
Waste mangt		3(2)	3(2)								
Decommissioning											

Table 5.9: Impact Ranking Table

Based on the ranking of consequence and likelihood as shown in the impact matrix table, a second matrix is compiled to calculate the overall significance of each of the identified potential impacts. This is referred to as the Significance Impact Matrix which is represented by a color coded 5 x 5 matrixes as shown below:

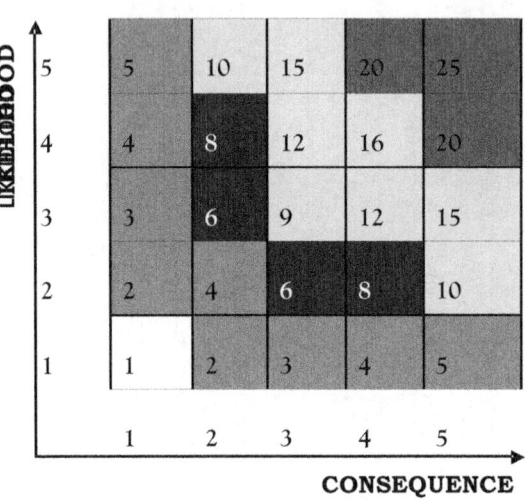

Fig 5.2 : 5x5 Matrix for consequence-likelihood product result

Based on the consequence-likelihood score (shown within the box as a product of consequence and likelihood), the impact scores are ranked into five categories in order of significance as illustrated

Ranking (consequence x likelihood)	Significance category
>16	Critical
9 - 16	High
6 - 8	Medium
2 - 5	Low
<2	Negligible

Table 5.10: Significance categorization

Based on this categorization, the product of the consequence and likelihood in the impact matrix table would indicate the severity level of the impact. For instance on table 5.9, the significance of impact of mobilization of equipment and material on surface water is 8 and this significance is interpreted as medium based on the categorization of the impact significance defined on table 5.7 a & b and Table 5.9

This ranking and categorization is done for all interactions and the summary is presented in a table as shown below:

Project Activities	Potential Impacts	Description	Consequence	Likelihood	Significance ranking
Land take	Loss of vegetation, exposure of top soil to erosion etc.	❖ Direct ❖ Negative ❖ Short term ❖ Local ❖ Reversible	Major	Minor	Moderate
		❖ Direct ❖ Negative ❖ Long term ❖ Widespread ❖ Reversible	High	low	Moderate

Table 5.11: Impact definition table

5.6. RESIDUAL IMPACT RANKING

The significance of impact is further determined following the introduction of feasible and cost effective mitigation measures to reduce the significance of the impact to acceptable levels. Given that mitigation measures are applied, an impact ranked high may present a residual low impact and a moderate impact may present a residual minor impact. Residual impact however is expected to be shown on the Environmental Management Plan (EMP) table that will be developed following presentation of the identified mitigation measures. Detailed discussions on impact mitigation and EMP are presented in chapters 6 and 7 respectively in this book.

5.7   Impact Description

Once the impact summary have been presented in a table as shown table 5.10 above, the next step is to present the description of the identified impacts in qualitative terms to support the quantitative assessment earlier conducted for the potential and associated impact in determining the impact significance.

The qualitative description of the identified impacts for each project activities enhances better understanding of the project impacts.

While quantitative assessment provides the platform for determining the risk level of the impact, qualitative description provides information on the impact i.e. description is the impact positive or negative (beneficial or adverse), short, medium or long term, localized, regional, national, international, reversible or irreversible, will the impact occur once, intermittently or continuously.

By so doing, we would be able to understand the nature, magnitude, frequency, aerial extent, duration, sensitivity and cumulative effect of the impact.

For the purpose of illustration, a qualitative description of the impact of mobilization of a typical project on the biophysical and socio-economic environment is presented below.

5.7.1 Impact of mobilization of personnel, materials and equipment

Mobilization will include labor/lifting, equipment and offloading of materials and equipment. Heavy duty and other equipment will be mobilized to and fro the construction site and may result in atmospheric emission of particulates and pollutant gases such as NO_x, SO_x, CO_2 etc.. Increase in ambient noise level, shoreline erosion, surface water contamination and pollution. Emission of pollutant gases may impact on the ambient air quality along mobilization route, this impact is however localized, short term and the concentration of these gases can be easily diluted by atmospheric air movement particularly if movement of vessels is in the early hours of the morning and late evening, the impact though negative is of low significance.

Movements of boats and vessels on the water way could result in disruption of fishing activities thereby affecting the livelihood of local fishermen. This impact though localized is of high significance as the economic activities of the fishermen will be significantly affected during the period of mobilization, so also the potential in local accidents increases due to the effect of wave actions generated by the bigger vessels conveying construction equipment, men and materials to and fro the construction site. This significance of this impact is critical considering the fact that a boat mishap could result in serious damages and fatalities.

The ripple/wave generated by the vessels conveying equipment, men and materials to and fro project site has the potential to create shore erosion along the coastline. This will no doubt aggravate the current problems of shoreline erosion facing the coastal communities along the transportation route.

This impact is of high significance considering the sensitivity of the fragile coastal line of the coastal communities around the area. Though the impact is localized, the effect is long term.

The description as shown above would be presented for all project related activities during construction, operations and decommissioning phases providing clear and concise description of the nature magnitude, duration etc.

NOTE: It must be noted that the qualitative description of the impacts must reflect the result of the quantitative evaluation. There must be correlation between the result of the quantitative assessment and qualitative description. As a matter of fact, the knowledge of impact description form the basis for quantitative assessment and the quantitative assessment is interpreted in qualitative description.

Impact Prediction

Prediction is the technical heart of environmental assessment and is an attempt to assist decision making on project options and alternative selections and reducing uncertainty with respect to accuracy of estimated impacts.

Methods for prediction cover a wide spectrum and cannot readily be categorized. All predictions are based on conceptual models of how the universe functions; they range in complexity from those that are totally intuitive to those based on explicit assumptions concerning the nature of environmental processes. Provided that the problem is well formulated and not too complex, scientific methods can be used, to obtain useful predictions, particularly in the biogeophysical disciplines. For example, given the climate (particularly the wind) at a representative site, together with information on time of day, topography and stack emission specifications, the patterns of ground level pollution concentrations around point source emission can be estimated (mean values for various averaging times, as well as frequency distributions).

Methods for predicting qualitative effects are difficult to find or to validate. In many cases, the prediction consists of indicating merely whether there will be degradation, no change, or enhancement of environmental quality. In other cases, quantitative ranking scales obtained in the impact ranking are used in predicting the quality effects/impacts of the activity as shown in section 5.7 above

Conclusion

Impact assessment requires that a multi-disciplinary team of experts in the relevant subject matters be constituted to systematically follow the established procedure and steps to consider and assess proposed project impacts on the ecological, aesthetic, cultural, historic, geological, economic, and social and health components of the project environmental.

There is no fast rule on the type of approach to be adopted for assessing the impact of a project but the critical thing to consider is that the methodologies chosen should be able to satisfy the requirements and expectations of impact assessment, no particular method can be recommended for impact assessment because project differs in their complexities and potentials to impact on the environment, also the environment is a dynamic system that is responding to natural processes and anthropogenic influences from time to time, the choice depends on how well the methodology satisfies the criteria earlier identified, as a matter of fact a combination of approach would best fulfill the objective of impact assessment and prediction.

Chapter Six

IMPACT
MITIGATION

Chapter six presents the guidance on developing cost effective impact mitigation measures that will be practicable and effective in mitigating or ameliorating projects, environmental and socio-economic impacts.

Impact Assessment is fundamentally an analysis of the changes to the bio-physical and socio-economic environment produced by a particular project or action. The earth which human inhabit with all other living and physical entities is constantly in a state of change to continually reach a balance of unanimity within the community. Because of the interaction and interrelationship of an earth's elements, every change produces associated changes. Most of the changes caused by living organisms however occur at an extremely slow rate. In contrast, changes produced as a result of human activities can occur rapidly and abruptly, for every change the process of reaching a new balance begin again.

Sometimes the results of anthropogenic changes are not beneficial and leave a surrounding environment that we neither wished for nor expected. Although developmental action/projects have good intent and solves or addresses some fundamental human needs, the resultant effect may be a degradation of the human environment beyond the benefit provided by the project, in order to ensure that developmental actions or project do not degrade the environment, mitigation measures are developed as controls/safeguards to mitigate/reduce the potential impact of the proposed action.

The study of and commitment to mitigation measures is an extensive and meaningful part of the EIA process. A development projects mitigation measures encompass all actions taken to eliminate, offset or reduce potentially adverse environmental impacts to acceptable levels (World Bank, 1999)

Mitigation measure according to the CEQ regulations is defined to follow this hierarchy:
I. Avoiding the impact e.g. through engineering design control.
II. Minimizing the impacts by limiting the degree or magnitude of the action. This could be done by changing project timing, location or layout engineering controls to minimize emission etc.
III. Rectifying the impact, repairing, rehabilitating or restoring the environment, impacted by unavoidable project impacts.
IV. Reducing or eliminating the impact over time.

V. Compensating for the impacts by replacing or providing substitute to resources or environment where non of the above practicable potentially adverse impacts can be avoided or mitigated to an acceptable levels through careful design and implementation (substitution could involve replacement of lost resources e.g. mangrove restoration, provision of financial services or any form of compensation) of appropriate measures or techniques to reduce the severity of the effects.

Mitigation measures may be broadly defined as either structural or non structural. Non structural measures include improvement to the legal or institutional framework, economic incentives (such as realistic pricing of utility services) training and measures to enhance public awareness. Structural measures encompass design or location changes engineered structures or landscape treatments based on the use of environmentally sound techniques and technologies (World Bank 1999).

The principle of prevention is better than cure applies to the mitigation measures development, this is because it is both easier and cheaper to avoid environmental impacts than try to rectify or reverse them. Basic prevention and avoidance principles of mitigation include:

1) Planning: this involves incorporating long-term environmental protection and safeguards or controls into project designs. This should include a structured process and cross functional team with appropriate expertise in the environmental issues of concern. The outcome of the risk assessment and impact evaluation conducted for the

project should guide the planning that is required upfront to avoid the identified impacts through a careful selection of best practicable designs and processes.

2) Limiting access to disturbed or highly sensitive areas. This requires that alternative project sites and routes to the proposed site or alternative means of transportation should be evaluated so as to avoid where practicable and minimize disturbance of undisturbed or sensitive ecological areas and historical cultural resources.

3) Minimizing physical and environmental foot-prints: site selection should be made with careful consideration of existing and adjacent land use, the sensitivity of the site should be taken into consideration so that project will be executed with minimum impact to conservation areas, landscape, wetlands, agricultural land, settlement etc. Typical land use/land cover map is shown in fig 6.1 and 6.2 below:

Fig 6.1: Schematic Landuse/Landcover Map (Not drawn to scale)

Fig 6.1: Schematic Landuse/Landcover Map (Not drawn to scale)

LEGEND
FARMLAND
FOREST RESERVE
VILLAGE SETLEMENT
WORSHIP CENTRE
BUSHES/SHRUBS
MARKET
COMMUNITY GARAGE
WATER BODY

Community Play Ground

Community Health Center

School Complex

PROPOSED PROJECT SITE

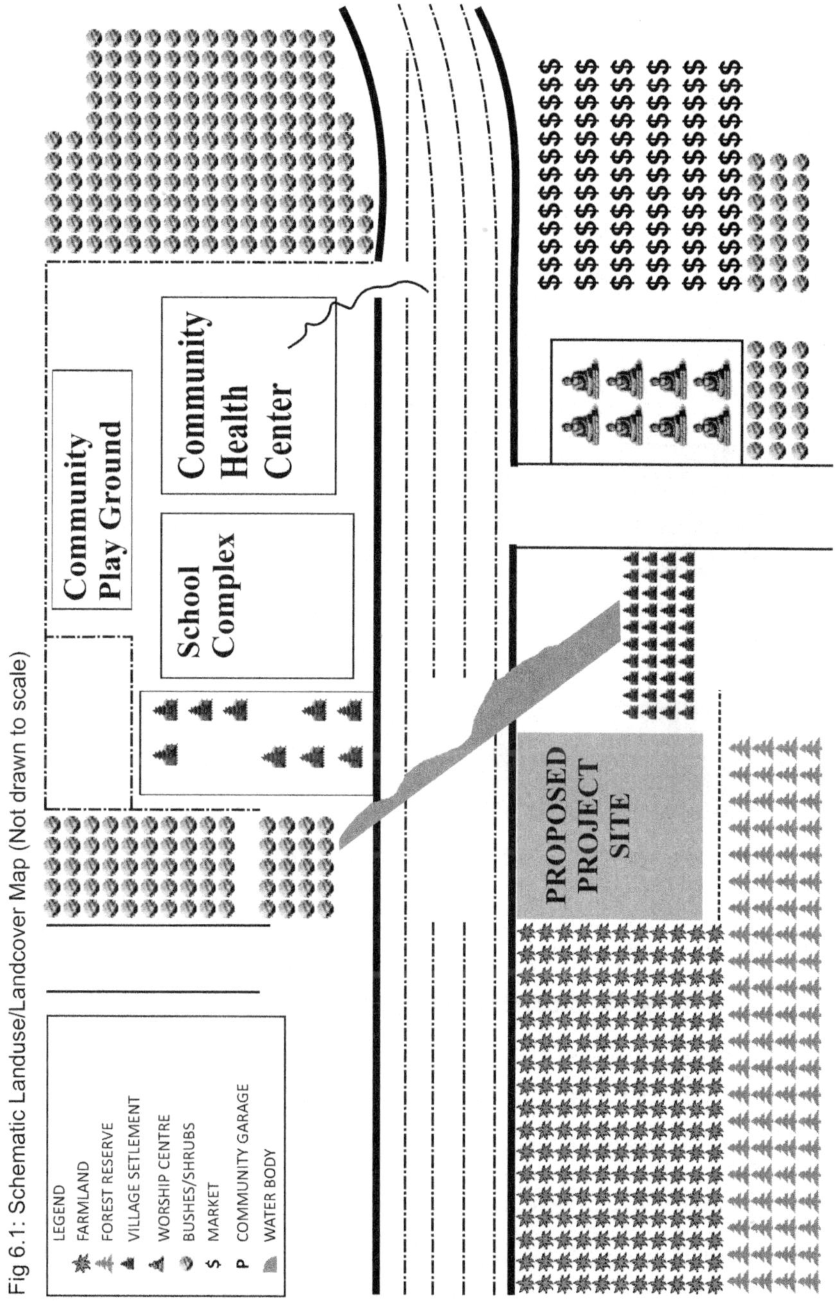

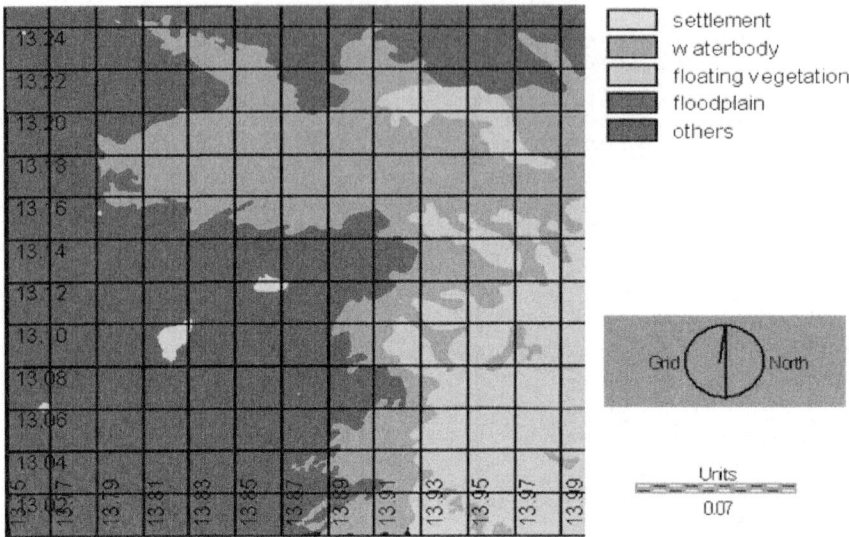

Fig 6.2:Landuse/Landcover Map of Lake Chad(1990)

Land take/Land use for project should be limited to the corridors that will guarantee minimum footprint e.g. pipeline right of way instead of creating a new route justified by distance and cost. Dredged spoils should be placed within bund walls instead of side casting or pumping into wetlands to prevent the spoils from eroding back to the canals with the potential to silt them up or create acidic run-off into the aquatic habitat, excavated materials should be properly stacked to reduce turbidity effects on run-off and run-off contained within existing storm water drainage system.

1) Maintaining natural conditions: this is particularly important with regards to hydrology especially in wetland

and aquatic habitats. Modifying hydrological systems can disrupt drainage system in highly dynamic environment and may yield surprising and often painful effects such as flooding, erosion, salt water intrusion. Therefore all designs should be focused on aligning with the natural drainage system.

2) Managing construction waste: this involves the development of project specific waste management plan upfront, the plan will take care of all emissions and releases into the environment and provides for a system for the proactive management of the entire waste stream that will be generated by the project during site preparation, construction, operation and decommissioning phases. By so doing the releases of solid liquids or gases wastes with high potential to contaminate and degrade the environment will be prevented.

In this section, let us consider some specific mitigation measures for some physical and socio-economic impact.

6.1 Wetland

Wetlands provide a wide variety of benefits to both nature and mankind. Wetlands are among the most productive areas of the earth. Their soil is extremely fertile and rich in biological diversity. The functional value of wetland is defined to include groundwater recharge, water quality of sedimentation, wildlife habitat, biological diversity, recreation and aesthetic. The contribution of wetlands to primary productivity, hydrological balance and the general environmental quality of the surrounding lands is as important as the total areas of wetlands. Ironically, wetland being fragile interface between land and water is highly vulnerable to human use, alteration and degradation with the pressure for development resulting in the loss of wetlands at alarming proportion.

To mitigate wetland impact, a three step sequence is recommended.

1) Avoidance
2) Minimization
3) Compensation
   a)   Restoration
   b)   Creation of human-made wetlands.

If a proposed project or action will involve the filling of wetlands, the first step in mitigation is development and evaluation of alternatives to avoid the wetland.

If avoidance is not possible, the analyst should evaluate all possible measures to minimize harm to the wetlands and its functional values.

Compensation including restoration of degraded wetlands or construction of replacement wetlands for those lost. Compensation actions should be considered only after all appropriate and applicable minimization options have be employed and adverse impact remains.

Restoration is preferred over creation of new wetlands because of the ever-present uncertainty of the success of created wetlands.

6.2 Restoration

For a project where construction would result in removal of riparian shrub habitat and grassland vegetation, it is recommended that restoration should be in the ratio of 2:1 i.e. 2 acres of riparian shrub habitat will be restored for each acre removed.

A specific riparian habitat restoration plan would be prepared and implemented having the following elements:

a. Planting native riparian trees and shrubs collected from local genetic stock.

b. Implementing necessary irrigation, weed control herbivore control and other cultivation measures for tree and shrub planting.

c. Establish habitat restoration success criteria based on achieving native vegetation cover and diversity and wildlife, habitat equal to greater than the habitat that was removed.

d. Initiating vegetation restoration and monitoring prior to removal of vegetation.

e. Monitoring the success of habitat restoration for at least 10 years.

f. Conducting a long term maintenance programme.

g. Establishing funding sources for long term maintenance and monitoring.

6.3 Creation of Wetlands

Off-site wetland creation normally involves converting an existing upland area to the type of wetland impacted or lost due to the proposed project or action. The design of mitigation or a compensatory wetland requires the coordinated efforts of hydrologists, geologists, engineers, and biologists.

Steps to creating human-made wetlands
Step 1: Locate a suitable site for the creation of replacement wetland: If a site is not available on or adjacent to the site of the proposed project then off-site locations will be considered.

Site selection should be based on characteristics that will enhance the probability of self-sustaining wetlands if possible as opposed to using upland areas, avoid complex hydraulic engineering features and/or questionable water sources that may create greater costs and higher risk of failure.

Step 2: Design the physical characteristics of the replacement wetland: After due   consideration has been given to the testing of soils and geology, the hydrology of the new site, detailed engineering construction plans and specifications are developed to indicate the required grading, excavation, soil replacement, location of dam etc.

Step 3:   Assessment of wetland species to be planted: The assessment should reflect the type and chemical, physical and biological functional values of the lost wetland, the assessment would include plant species composition and diversity, this will provide information required for vegetation selection based on wildlife cover nesting site, wildlife food etc. A vegetation plan is then developed with the grading plan to indicate what species should be planted at what location by grouping/composition and distribution.

6.4 Vegetation and Wildlife Impact Mitigation

The level of details required for impact analysis and mitigation for vegetation and wildlife will depend on the specific characteristics of the proposed project alternatives and the expected degree of impacts. The types of impact that may be generated include: loss of unique vegetation communities direct loss of wildlife and habitat, barriers to wildlife travel corridors and effects on recreational activities.

Mitigation for potential impacts on vegetation and wildlife may be site-specific, such as replacing landscaping, clearing of vegetation in batches and establishment of buffer zone, in some cases, rare plants or particular animal species may be transplanted or trapped and moved to other locations out of harm way limiting site clearance to only areas required for project development and replacement of loss vegetation offsite or creating parks in urban areas.

The mitigation measures considered above are basically the same following the principles of mitigation:
  I.   Avoiding
  II. Minimizing
  III. Rectifying

IV.   Reducing

V.   Compensating

6.5   Air Impact Mitigation

Air pollution according to the World Bank is the presence in the atmosphere of one or more contaminants (such as dust, fumes, gas, mist, odor, smokes or vapor) in such quantities, characteristics and duration as to make them actually or potentially injurious to human, plant or animal life or to property or which unreasonably interfere with the comfortable enjoyment of life and property (World Bank 1978)

Because air pollution can directly cause health risks to the human population, improvement of the quality has been an important goal of environmental legislation and regulation. For instance, the Nigerian National Air Quality Standard stipulates the allowable concentration of air pollutants in the atmosphere and expects every activity that would result in air emissions and pollution be conducted within the target limits of the pollutants.

To develop effective mitigation measures, certain information are required, they include:

a) Identify air pollutants associated with the project activities including sources of pollution.

b) Describe existing air quality levels.

c) Describe the basic meteorological data such as temperature, wind speed and direction, precipitation etc.

d) Assemble information on air pollution dispersion characteristics.

e) Understand the legislative and regulatory requirements on air quality standard.

With the foregoing information, successful measures for reducing harmful emission into the atmosphere can be developed. Among the generally used mitigation measures are:

a. Use of equipment with high combustion efficiency.

b. Use of solar-powered or gas powered engine rather than diesel powered engines.

c. Cleaning of flue gases with inertial separators fabric filters, scrubbers or electrostatic precipitators to reduce emission of total suspended particulate (TSP).

d. Automobile engines modification proper turning, exhaust gas recirculation, redesign of combustion chamber (catalytic or thermal devices) regular engine maintenance.

e. Optimization of journey trips to reduce emission from mobile sources.

f. Use of low NOX burners.

6.6 Socio-economic Impact Mitigation

Project development and execution generates both beneficial and adverse socio-economic impacts. Though project specific, the negative impacts may include: cultural interference and conflict, employee immigration and resultant increase in population and pressure on existing infrastructural facilities, increase in crime and social vices (such as prostitution, post construction economic burst and attendant social-unrest, social dislocation and sectoral shift from traditional occupation to unskilled labor force, inter and intra community tension, disruption of community means of livelihood such as disturbance of fishing ground, agricultural land etc.) nuisance and noise induced psychological stress, archeological or religious site impact etc.

The development of possible mitigation measures is often project specific. In all cases, the affected communities and other stakeholders should be consulted and informed of the preliminary results of impact analysis to then develop a set of possible mitigation techniques or actions. The list of possible measures must be evaluated for effectiveness and feasibility.

For the purpose of illustration, the following general mitigation measures have been developed for some of the impacts earlier identified above.

Pressure on existing facilities: Information on estimated number of construction worker can be used in prediction of anticipated workers influx and the resultant increase in population can be offset by early planning for adequate infrastructure to meet the needs of an increased population and not cause undue pressure on available infrastructural facilities. Often the sponsor of the proposed project or action can create project specific road ways or other facilities if it is agreed upon early enough, alternatively the project construction work force can be accommodated within the boundary of the project site in a closed camp system whereby there will be no interaction between the project workers and the community.

Land use/Land values: mitigation of predicted land value impacts most often is project specific and involves the design elements of the proposed project or surrounding parcel of land such as landscaping to create visual barriers staggered work hours to avoid localized traffic congestion avoidance of odor impact, public enlightenment, public meetings can also offset the perception on adverse land value/impacts.

Generally, all measures to make the facility a "better neighbor" will assist in reducing any negative impact to land values in adjacent area.

Post construction employment burst: some project development activities result in the employment of thousands of community youths for various skilled, semi-skilled and unskilled job functions during construction phase. While this in itself is a beneficial impact, the disengagement of the construction workers at the end of construction activities will create a pool of unmeployed youths that if not proactively managed would constitute a source of tension for the project and the society. To mitigate this impact, the project need to develop training, skill acquisition and empowerment programs targeted at preparing the construction workers for post construction life.

Consistent with the requirement of labour law, disengagement allowances are expected to be paid to the construction workers when disengaged and demobilized. There should necessarily be training and workshops organized for the workers to ensuring that they optimize their post construction life for benefit of the project and the society.

The mitigation measures discussed above are not exhaustive; few illustrations were only given to boost understanding on the subject of impact mitigation.

NOTE: It is important to note that a cross functional evaluation is required in developing mitigation measures, this is because mitigation measures may have environmental and socio-economic and health dimension such that mitigating one problem may create another concerns, i.e solving one problem to create another e.g establishing a closed camp for project workers to avoid pressure on existing community infrastructure may limit economic transaction that can boost local economic development thereby creating tension for contract and employment.

Off-site wetland creation normally involves converting an existing upland area to the type of wetland impacted or lost due to the proposed project or action; this can result in fragmentation of arable farmland for subsistence agriculture and its attendant socio-economic effects. Also creating an alternative project specific road to avoid traffic congestion/accident, limit air emissions within the community may disconnect the community from deriving full benefits from road usage and revenue generation.

At any rate, compensating for lost of beneficial use remains the fundamental philosophy that drives the principles of impact mitigation.

Chapter Seven

ENVIRONMENTAL
MANAGEMENT PLAN (EMP)

This chapter discusses the elements of an Environmental Management Plan (EMP), and the requirements for implementing the EMP to deriving the values it adds to EIA as a management tool for ensuring project sound environmental performance.

The DPR EGASPIN (2002) defines EMP as planned and integrated environmental management practice, aimed at ensuring that unforeseen, identified and unidentified environmental issues are contained and brought to acceptable levels. The EMP is a critical component of an impact assessment process. It is an important tool that can be used to continuously measure and check the efficacy of the mitigation measures recommended by the impact assessment.

The FMEnv EIA sectoral Guideline requires that an EMP must be integrated into the EIA process as it provides the means for continuous self-assessment of the predicted accuracy of the impacts and the management effectiveness of management strategies for sound project implementation and operation.

According to World Bank, 1999, A project environmental management plan outlines the mitigation, monitoring and institutional measures to be taken during the project construction, operation and decommissioning phases to avoid or control adverse environmental and social impacts, offset them or reduce them to acceptable levels.

The EMP is a tool developed to provide the mechanism for implementing the commitment on environmental protection in the Environmental Impact Assessment (EIA. It is also a proactive action designed to monitor potential environmental impact resulting from the project with objective of minimizing and mitigating their effects on the environment.

The value of the EIA is in the implementation of the EMP, if the EMP is not implemented the aim of EIA is defeated. The implementation of the EMP is the engine that drives the EIA to achieve its objectives.

Environmental management includes protection, conservation, mitigation, and enhancement measures as well as monitoring.

FMEnv Requirement
The National EIA Procedure issued by the FMEnv stipulates that:
- Prior to commissioning, i.e. during the implementation of the (new) project, the Agency (FMEnv) shall monitor the progress of the project from site preparation to commissioning in order to ensure compliance with all stipulated mitigation measures and project specifications.
- Also, a post-commissioning audit that involves periodic assessment of the positive and negative impacts of the

project shall be conducted   (by the Agency) to help improve the EIA process

DPR Requirement

The DPR EGASPIN (2002) provides basic requirement for the implementation of EMP (Post-EIA Monitoring): Post EIA Monitoring shall be designed and implemented to:

- Document impacts that result from a proposed project/activity/action, to predict more accurately project/activity/action;
- Forewarn the DPR and/or the proponent of unanticipated adverse impacts or sudden changes in impact trends and provide immediate warning whenever an impact indicator approaches a critical level. In the interim, the critical levels can be defined in terms of:
  - o   Carrying Capacity
  - o   Threshold Levels
  - o   Regulation and Enforcement Standards
- Potentially control and manage the timing, location and level of impacts and;
- Provide the cause and effect data for the empirical verification or validation of various predictive models of action/impact relationships.

7.1   Goals of EMP Implementation/Monitoring

Impact monitoring in the context of FEPA EIA procedure (1995) is the activity undertaken to identify variation in environmental parameters which can be attributed with confidence to the presence of a project or other causes. Its to identify project induced changes to assist in the management of environmental effects by observing the extent of change and degree of mitigation which is necessary

7.2 Objectives of EMP

(a) To establish whether or not the project activities are compliant with regulatory standards and recommended mitigation measures in the EIA report to support management initiatives to improve environmental performance.

(b) Monitor alterations in existing physical, chemical and biological characteristics of the environment

(c) Determine if any detected changes in the environmental components are caused by the project activities or natural occurrences.

(d) Provide evidence of compliance and non-compliance.

(e) Determine the effectiveness of the ameliorating measures.

(f) Provide a safe guide against liability claims from past practice and mitigate long-term liability.

(g) Provide early warning of any potentially significant problems.

Above objectives can be summarized with the following
* Mitigation of project environmental and social risks
* Ensuring regulatory compliance
* Avoid delays
* Avoid liabilities and litigations

7.3 Attributes of an EMP

Based on ISO 14001 EMS, the attributes of an EMP include:

1) **Policy:** The environmental policy statement that establishes an overall framework for the development of appropriate environmental objectives and targets that are aligned with the project bussines objectives

2) **Planning:** Environmental objectives and targets are established based primarily on regulatory requirements and associated environmental impacts as determined in the EIA.

3) **Operational Control:** Appropriate controls for achieving the environmental objectives and targets will be established through auditing requirement of the EMP, standard operating procedures and processes and systems. Operational control is enabled with a clear organizational structure assigned environmental roles, responsibilities, training, thorough documentation of environmental activities

4) **Monitoring and Measurement:** An environmental monitoring programme will be implemented to ensure full compliance with regulations and verify the effectiveness of the impact mitigation activities

5) **Management Review:** In addition to the regular internal and external audits conducted during monitoring and measurement, an annual review by the project management is expected to determine performance gaps and response action in closing out those gaps. This review will focus on revising the environmental objectives and targets and allocation of funds for new impact mitigation and training

7.4. Components of an EMP

Based on the World Bank's recommendation on EMP as adopted from the Environmental Source Book Update (1999), the following aspects should typically be addressed within an EMP

a) **Summary of impacts:** The predicted adverse environmental and social impacts for which mitigation is required should be identified and briefly summarized. Cross – referencing to the impact assessment section of the

EIA and other documentation is recommended so that additional details can readily be referenced .

b) **Description of mitigation measures:** The EMP identifies feasible and cost effective measures to reduce potentially significant environmental and social impacts to acceptable levels. Each mitigation measure should briefly describe with reference to the impact to which it relates and the condition under which is required(for example, continuously or in the event of contingencies). These should be accompanied by or reference to design, equipment description and operating procedures which elaborates on the technical aspects of implementing the various measures. Where mitigation measures may result in secondary impacts, their significance should be evaluated.

c) **Description of monitoring program:** Environmental performance measurement should be designed to ensure that mitigation measures are implemented, have the intended results and that remedial measures are undertaken if mitigation measures are inadequate or the impacts have been underestimated within the EIA report. It should assess compliance with national and international standards and regulatory requirements. The monitoring program should clearly indicate the linkage between impacts identified in the EIA report, indicators to be measured, method to be used, sampling locations, frequency of measurement, detection limits(where applicable) and definition of thresholds that will signal the need for corrective action etc

d) **Institutional arrangements:** Responsibilities for mitigation and monitoring should be clearly defined. The EMP should identify arrangements for coordination between the various actors responsible for mitigation e.g between the regulatory bodies and the project owner.

e) **Implementation schedule and reporting procedure:** The timing , frequency and duration of mitigation measures should be specified in an implementation schedule showing links with the overall project implementation plan. Procedures to provide information on the progress and results of mitigation and monitoring measures should also be clearly specified. As a minimum, the recipients of such information should include those with responsibilities for ensuring timely implementation of mitigation measures and for undertaking remedial actions in response to branches of monitoring thresholds, such parties include the regulatory agencies, Project Manager, Construction/Site Manager, Safety and Environment Manager, Public Affairs Manager etc.

f) **Cost estimates/Budget:** The estimated cost for both intial investment and recurrent expenses for implementing all measures contained in the EMP should be specified and integrated into the overall project cost and also into loan negotiation document when funding is to be sourced from external sources. Environmental assessment cost rarely exceed one percent(1%) of the total capital cost of the project and is frequently less than that. The cost of implementing mitigation measures can range from 3 to 10 percent of total project cost with 3- 5 percent being common. These estimates do not take into account possible cost savings that result from implementing the mitigation recommendation that reduce or avoid the cost of violations of environmental objectives.

The EMP components discussed above can be represented in a table format clearly presenting the expectation of each of the aspects. The table below gives an illustration of an environmental monitoring plan desirable from the components discussed above.

Project Activity	Potential Impact	Receptor	Impact ranking	Mitigation measures	Residual impact ranking	Regulatory compliance monitoring	Effect monitoiring	Monitoring parameters	Frequency of monitoring	Responsible party

Table 7.1: Typical Environmental Management Plan Table

Meanwhile, it is important to state here that there is no standard format for EMPs. Once the format takes into account the EMP components discussed above, it can be designed to be fit for purpose to fit the circumstances for which the EMP is being developed and the requirements for which its designed to meet among others

The factors that will influence the format of the EMP is summarized under the following:
- Baseline condition
- Project scope
- Impact significance
- Regulatory requirement
- Funding
- Regulatory enforcement

Essentially, the EMP should detail all plans and processes that would enable the project proponent meet the commitments that have been made on impact mitigation in order to ensure that projects are implemented in an environmentally sound manner

7.5.EMP Implementation/Post EIA Monitoring
If the EMP is a critical component of the EIA, the implementation of the EMP requirement is the singular most important factor that determines the level to which the EIA will achieve its set objectives.

The resources and energy committed to conducting environmental assessment will amount to nothingness if the EMP is not implemented or not effectively implemented.

Therefore the value of an EIA will only be realized when the EMP commitments and obligations are fully implemented

The United Nation Environment Programme defined Environmental monitoring as the systematic collection of environmental data through repetitive measurement(UNEP,

1996). It describes three known types of environmental monitoring within the conceptual environmental impact assessment framework as follows:

1. **Baseline monitoring:** This refers to the measurement of environmental parameters in the pre-project period

2. **Effect monitoring:** Involves the measurements of environmental parameters during project construction and implementation phase so as to detect changes in the parameters which can be attributed to the project

3. **Compliance monitoring:** This is the periodic or continuous measurement of environmental parameters or discharges to ensure that regulatory requirements and standards are met. Compliance monitoring can further be broken down into two, namely:

   a) Mitigation measures monitoring which relates to the prescribed mitigation measures in the EIA

   b) Regulatory compliance monitoring which relates to existing regulatory monitoring requirements

The baseline data is the basis for which the effect and compliance monitoring will be compared in establishing the shift and variation in environmental characteristics and qualities

The above stated attributes of an EMP encapsulated in the organization EMS is further corroborated by the DPR EGASPIN 2002 that requires that organization shall establish and maintain a monitoring program that establishes the specifics of the environmental and socio-economic monitoring parameters for each component of the environment that may be affected by the project. The component usually includes:

- Atmosphere (Air quality and Noise)
- Surface and ground water
- Vegetation and wildlife
- Soil
- Socio-economic and public health
- Waste management
- Traffic and transportation
- Personnel health and safety, etc

Regular data collection, audits, inspections, and related monitoring activities are conducted for each category at a pre-determined frequency, either based on the schedule established in the regulations for Regulatory Monitoring or based on the EIA monitoring schedule established specifically for the project.

In conducting impact mitigation monitoring, independent consultants are engaged with the participation of the relevant regulatory agencies e.gFMEnv, state ministry of environment and DPR if the project is oil and gas related.

The essence is to obtain independent judgment on environmental quality and performance within and around project zone of influence. Any non comformance or variation in environemtal qualities from baseline conditions are communicated to the proponent for corrective actions to be taken to mitigate or remediate or restore the damaged environment. By so doing, the functioning of the ecological processes will be sustained.

Chapter Eight

STAKEHOLDERS ENGAGEMENT
AND PUBLIC CONSULTATION

> *This chapter presents stakeholders consultation and
> engagement as a critical activity of the EIA process and its
> relevance in defining the quality of the EIA and project
> acceptability by a network of stakeholders.*

In the EIA process, stakeholders engagement and public consultation is a critical element that enhances the value of the EIA, this is because the sustainability of a project is largely influenced by the level of support from the project stakeholders

Who are stakeholders? They are simply people that are impacted by the project or could impact the project, they could be internal to the organization such as the different functional units that would influence decisions on the project or external parties such as the project community/communities, government regulatory agencies, NGOs etc.

Stakeholder engagement is the process by which an organization involves people who may be affected by the decisions it makes or can influence the implementation of its decisions in the project implementation process. They may support or oppose the decisions, be influential in the organization or within the community in which it operates, holds relevant official positions or be affected in the long term.

It is a requirement of the World Bank as stated in the Bank's Operational Directive (OD) 4.01 on environmental assessment that affected groups and non-governmental organizations(NGOs) be consulted as part of the environmental assessment of projects. Its also a requirement of the International Finance Corporation (IFC) as stated in Performance Standard 1 that effective community engagement through disclosure of project related information and consultation with local communities should be carried out as part of assessing the social and environmental sustainability of a project.

The primary purpose of these provisions is to protect the interests of the affected communities, especially the poor and the vulnerable.

It is critical that public concerns are recognized at an early stage of the project environmental assessment planning, this is so because public views and perceptions of the project are critical to the successful implementation and operation of the project. A project may have obtained all the relevant permits and approvals from the government to implement a project but may not be able to execute the project if the project communities have not given their support and goodwill popularly known as the "social licence" to execute the project. Community hostilities, resistances, conflicts and crises would normally be experienced where the social licence to execute the project has not been given by the project communities.

To ensure that community issues and concerns are adequately identified and addressed, stakeholders engagement should cover the entire life cycle of the EIA i.e screening, scoping, impact assessment and EMP development and implementation, this is because, community expectations are dynamic and are constantly changing.

Experience has shown that projects with a robust and effective stakeholder's engagement and public consultations are more successfully implemented than those with shallow engagement and consultation. It must be noted that projects that are weak in stakeholders engagement and public consultations face more social risks that could significantly impact on project implementation schedule and operations and ultimately on the company's reputation.

Also, Stakeholder engagement is a key part of corporate social responsibility (CSR) philosophies. Companies engage their stakeholders in dialogue to find out what social and environmental issues matter most to them about their performance in order to improve decision-making and accountability. Engaging stakeholders is a requirement of the

Global Reporting Initiative, a network-based organisation with sustainability reporting framework that is widely used around the world.

Involving stakeholders in decision-making processes is not confined to corporate social responsibility (CSR) processes. It's a tool used by private and public sector organizations, especially when they want to develop understanding and agree to solutions on complex issues or issues of concern.

An underlying principle of stakeholder engagement is that stakeholders have the chance to influence the decision-making process. This differentiates stakeholder engagement from communications processes that seek to issue a message or influence groups to agree with a decision that is already made. The Environment Council developed the Principles of Authentic Engagement. These are intended to provide a framework for genuine stakeholder engagement.

The practitioners in stakeholder engagement are often businesses, non-governmental organizations (NGOs), labor organizations, trade and industry organizations, governments, and financial institutions

8.1 Benefits of Stakeholders Engagement and Public Consultation
   a) Stakeholder engagement provides opportunities to further align business practices with societal needs and expectations, helping to drive long-term sustainability and shareholders value

b) Stakeholders can influence the project to reduce adverse impacts, maximize benefits and ensure that they receive appropriate attention

c) Involvement of the communities at early stages (Screening and Scoping) of the EIA enhances timely disclosure of relevant information to all stakeholders

d) Stakeholders concerns are captured early and are reflected in the project decisions such as design, site selection, alternative selection etc.

e) Enhances the quality of decision making by government and project proponent

f) Reduces or eliminate conflicts and delays thereby improving profitability to investors

g) Greater sound platform for development of effective environmental management plan

h) Enhances company's reputation and corporate image.

Although the monetary cost of stakeholders engagement could be high, the cost of failing to consult stakeholders will quadruple the cost of engagement, for instance, one of the consequences of failing to identify with and consult stakeholders is long lasting unwarranted hostilities to the project that will result in huge spending on security, conflict resolution, reputation management and lost time cost.

8.2   Elements of Stakeholders Engagement

There are three key elements of stakeholders engagement as shown below

a) Stakeholders Engagement Plan :

Before developing an engagement strategy, it is important to first understand what stakeholder engagement means to your company. The stakeholders engagement plan defines philosophy of the company stakeholders engagement plans with respect to the planned project and outline the strategy of engagement, resources required, roles and responsibilities for engagement activities etc.

The plan presents the strategy that will be implemented to effectively capture all relevant actions and communications on stakeholders engagement for the project.

b) Stakeholders Mapping

Stakeholder mapping is a collaborative process of research, debate, and discussion that draws from multiple perspectives to determine a key list of stakeholders across the entire stakeholder spectrum

Mapping is an important step to understanding who your key stakeholders are, where they come from, and what they are looking for in relationship to your business. Mapping can be broken down into four phases:

I. Identifying: listing relevant groups, organizations, and people
II. Analyzing: understanding stakeholder perspectives and relevance
III. Mapping: visualizing relationships to objectives and other stakeholders
IV. Prioritizing: ranking stakeholder relevance and identifying issues

The process of stakeholder mapping is as important as the result, and the quality of the process depends heavily on the knowledge of the people participating.

Stakeholders mapping defines criteria for identifying and prioritizing stakeholders of the project and their degree of influence.

Mapping allows you to see where stakeholders stand to determine which stakeholders are most useful to engage with. when evaluated by the same key criteria and compared to each other and helps you visualize the often complex interplay of issues and relationships created in the criteria chart

c) Stakeholders analysis

Once you have identified a list of stakeholders, it is useful to do further analysis to better understand their relevance and the perspective they offer, to understand their relationship to the issue(s) and each other, and to prioritize based on their relative usefulness for this engagement . Shown below is the list of criteria adapted from BSR (2011) to help you analyze each identified stakeholder

I.   **Contribution:** Does the stakeholder have information, counsel, or expertise on the issue that could be helpful to the company/project?

II.   **Legitimacy:** How legitimate is the stakeholder's claim for engagement?

III. **Willingness to engage:** How willing is the stakeholder to engage?

IV.   **Influence:** How much influence does the stakeholder have? (You will need to clarify "who" they influence, e.g., other companies, NGOs, consumers, investors, etc.)

V.   **Necessity of involvement:** Is this someone who could derail or delegitimize the process if they were not included in the engagement?

These five criteria are used to create and populate a chart with short descriptions of how stakeholders fulfill them assigning values of low, medium, or high each stakeholders to determine the relevance of a particular stakeholder and the level of engagement that is required

8.3   Stakeholders consultation

Communication is established between the proponent and identified stakeholders on project related information and impact assessment. The engagement is conducted to ensuring equitable stakeholder contribution and mitigating tension while remaining focused on the issues on stakeholder expectations: Share feedback from earlier goal-setting consultation process, or open the floor to stakeholders to share their expectations for the engagement. The facilitator planning to facilitate the event, must be sure to focus on the following points

I. Allow for equal contribution: Encourage the stakeholders to participate in the conversation; create a space where this is possible and comfortable; respect each party's opinion and views of the issue being discussed.

II. Focus on the discussion: Dialogues can veer off-topic if not properly focused. Stick to your agenda and remain within the scope of the issue. Table any out-of-scope issues for future engagements, and be sure to address these in the future if you commit to doing so.

III. Manage cultural dynamics: Earlier activities should have prepared the facilitator for any tricky dynamics. But be wary of possible cultural misunderstandings during engagement, and manage them as they arise.

IV. Mitigate tension: Certain topics can be controversial or provocative, and there may be unexpected dynamics or rivalries between participants. Have security on-site to address elevated situations, but pre-empt difficulties by maintaining a calm atmosphere in the room.

Document the engagement and develop action plan: In order to measure success and build on your efforts for future activities, make sure to capture the following in writing during the engagement: the original purpose and aims of the engagement, the methods used, the participants, a summary of noted stakeholder concerns, expectations and perceptions, a summary of discussions, and a robust list of outputs (decisions, actions, proposals, and recommendations).Identify opportunities from feedback and determine actions, revisit goals and plan next steps for follow-up and future engagement

8.4   Stakeholder Engagement Methods & Tactics

Stakeholder engagement methods are the means by which stakeholders are involved in decision-making and stakeholder views and opinions are sought. There is no single method to involve stakeholders in any given decision, and in many cases, a number of alternative methods will be employed, sequentially or in combination, to ensure an effective flow of information.

Stakeholder engagement methods can include
· Field surveys using questionnaires and interview
· face-to-face meetings (individual or group)
· Focused group discussion
· Telephone conversation/ online meetings

Tactics are high-level descriptions of how you approach stakeholders. This approach can be simplified into three categories: engage, communicate, and inform:

Engage describes stakeholders with whom engagement is necessary.

Communicate describes stakeholders with a high willingness to engage or a high level of expertise but who have not yet participated in dialogue with your company. Communicating more with these stakeholders will help them value engagement.

Conclusion

Influencers from the community, government, civil society, and the private sector play an important role in creating and maintaining business value. As their influence evolves, companies must take a strategic and structured approach to stakeholder relations and management. Early involvement of the stakeholders(internal and external) in the EIA process provides a veritable platform for stakeholders issue, concerns and expectations to be captured and addressed in order to promote the sustainability of the project.

Bibliography

Adcroft, A., R. Hallberg, J. P. Dunne, B. L. Samuels, J. A. Galt, C. H. Barke, and D. Payton (2010). "Simulations of underwater plumes of dissolved oil in the Gulf of Mexico" . Geophysical Research Letters Shirley, Thomas C.; John

Adeniyi P. O. (1998). Making remote Sensing and GIS work for sustainable Agriculture and rural development in sub-Sahara Africa, in Geoinformation Technology Applications for Resource and Environmental management in Africa . AARSE, UNILAG Lagos.

Alfa N. I. (2003). Monitoring Extent of Changes in Surface Water in Lake Chad using Remote Sensing Data from 1963 to 2000.Newsletter of the National Centre for Remote Sensing Vol. 1.No. 2. NCRS, Jos.

Anderson, B. (1967). Report on the Soils of the Niger Delt Area. Niger Delta

Angermeier P. L. and Bailey, A. (1991). Use of Geographic Information System as a Conservation Tool of Rivers in Virginia USA; FAO Technical Paper no 318 FAO Rome.

Asigbaase M, 2012: Areview of Global Environmental Impact Assessment (EIA) practice. Ambassador Michael Publishers, USA

Betty Bowers Marriot (1997), Environmental Impact Assessment: A practical Guide, McGraw-Hill Publishers, New York.

Brandon Keim (March 24, 2009). "The Exxon Valdez Spill Is All Around Us". Wired Science. Retrieved June 29, 2010

Broughton, Edward (2005). "The Bhopal disaster and its aftermath: a review". Environmental Health ,Columbia University Press, New York, USA.

Burrough, P. A. (1986). Principle of Geographical information systems for Land Resources Assessment, Oxford University Press: Oxford.

Canter, L. W. (1996). Environmental Impact Assessment. Second Edition, New York, USA: McGraw Hill

Canters, K., ed. (1997), Habitat fragmentation and infrastructure. The Hague: Ministry of Transport, Public Works and Water Management

Carmouze, J. P. (1971). Hydrological Regulation of the Water of Lake Chad. Trav. Dops. RSTOM 58. Fish Farming International.

Cheng, C. and Jan. J. (2004). Application of GIS to measure and Evaluate Landscape Changes, Taiwan Forestry Research Institute, Taiwan.

David Sive, Mark A, Chertok Sive and Riesel P.C (2005): Little NEPAs and their Environmental Impact Assessment Process : http://www.sprlaw.com/pdf/spr_little_nepa_ali_aba_0605

Deepwater Horizon Marine Casualty Investigation Report (2011). Office of the Maritime Administrator, 17 August, in http://www.register iri.com/forms/ upload/Republic_of_the_Marshall_Islands_DEEPWATER_HORIZ ON_Marine_Casualty_Investigation_Report-Low_Resolution.pdf. Retrieved 25 February 2013

Department of Petroleum Resource (2002). Environmental Guidelines and Standards for the Petroleum Industry in Nigeria, Ministry of Petroleum Resources, Lagos

Eccleston, Charles; Doub, J. Peyton (2012). Preparing NEPA Environmental Assessments: A User's Guide to Best Professional Practices. CRC Press,

Eckerman, Ingrid (2001). Chemical Industry and Public Health: Bhopal as an Example. Gothenburg, Sweden: Nordic School of Public Health.

Eckerman, Ingrid (2005). The Bhopal Saga—Causes and Consequences of the World's Largest Industrial Disaster. India: Universities Press.

Eckerman, Ingrid (2013). Bhopal Catastrophe 1984: Causes and Consequences (in Reference Module in Earth Systems and Environmental Sciences). Elsevier

Eckerman, Ingrid (2013). Bhopal Catastrophe 1984: Causes and Consequences. Encyclopedae of Environment Health. Elsevia, India

Elliott, M. & Thomas, I. (2009), "Environment Impact Assessment in Australia: Theory and Practice, 5th Edn, Federation Press, Sydney.

Equator Principles (2006). Environmental and social Risk Management for Project Financing in http://www.equator-principles.com/index.php/governance-and-management.

FAO (1991)--- GIS Thesis.
Federal Environmental Protection Agency (1991).

Guidelines and Standard for Environmental Control in Nigeria, Lagos
Federal Environmental Protection Agency (1992). EIA Decree 86 (1992). Federal Republic of Nigeria, Lagos

Federal Environmental Protection Agency (1999). National Guidelines on Environmental Audit in Nigeria. FEPA Decree No 14 of 1999. Federal Republic of Nigeria

Federal Environmental Protection Agency (1989). National Policy on the Environment. The Presidency, Abuja, Nigeria

Gerald Foley(1991). Global Warming.Who is taking the Heat? Panos Publication.London UK

Graham, Sarah (2003). "Environmental Effects of Exxon Valdez Spill Still Being Felt", Scientific American. Retrieved March 9, 2008.
http://www.uscg.mil/dwh_report (2013). On Scene Coordinator Report on Deepwater Horizon Oil Spill (Report)
http://www.ieso.ca/imoweb/consult/stakeholder methods-process.asp
http://www.wikipedia.org: Stakeholder engagement
http://www.bsr.org/reports/BSR () "Five –step Guide to Stakeholder Engagement"
http://en.wikipedia.org/wiki/Environmental_chemistry
http://en.wikipedia.org/wiki/Minamata_disease
http://en.wikipedia.org/wiki/Itai-itai_disease
http://en.wikipedia.org/wiki/Love_Canal
http://en.wikipedia.org/wiki/Bhopal_disaster
http://en.wikipedia.org/wiki/Exxon_Valdez_oil_spill
http://www.abc.net.au/news/2006-05-17/exxon-valdez-oil-spill-still-a-threat-study.

http://www.pbs.org/newshour/updates/25-years-later-scientists-remember-exxon-valdez-spill
http://en.wikipedia.org/wiki/Deepwater_Horizon_oil_spill
http://www.npr.org/for-bp-cleanup-2013
http://www.tampabay.com/news/environment/water/oil-from-bp-spill
http://news.discovery.com/animals/whales-dolphins/record-dolphin-sea-turtle-deaths-since-gulf-spill
http://www.reuters.com/article/2010/us-oil-spill-carcinogens
http://elr.info/litigation sierra-club-v-corps-engrs: The Environmental Law Reporter. Sierra Club V. Corps of Engr, Citation: 13 ELR 20326

Institute of Development Economy (1994). Environmental Law in Developing Countries, Southeast and East Asia, Development and Environment Series 6,

International Finance Corporation (2006). Performance Standards on Social and Environmental Sustainability

ISO 14001 (2014), Environmental Management Systems. International Organization for Standardization, Geneva, Switzerland.

Jewett SC, Dean TA, and Hoberg M(2001). "Scuba Techniques Used to Assess the Effects of the Exxon Valdez Oil Spill". In: SC Jewett (ed). Cold Water Diving for Science. Proceedings of the American Academy of Underwater Sciences, 21st Annual Scientific Diving Symposium.

Leopold, L. B., Clarke, F. E., Henshaw, B. B. and Balsley, J. R. (1971) A Procedure for Evaluating Environmental Impacts: Geological Survey Circular 645. Washington: Government Print Office

Lan McHarg (1968), Overlay Maps and the Evaluation of Social and Environmental Costs of Land Use Change, Center for Spatially Integrated Social Science. Island Press, Washington DC.

Michael Horsefall (2011). Chemistry and Heavy Metals are Janus – Faced, Inaugural Lecture Series, No 81, Delivered at the University of Port Harcourt, Rivers State, Nigeria

National Institute for Minamata Disease (2001). Minamata Disease Archives. Ministry of the Environment, Japan

National Research Council (1991), Environmental Epidemiology, vol. 1: Public Health and Hazardous Wastes National Academy Press .Washington:

Omoyeni, Bernard (2005). Evaluation of Wetland Ecosystem Changes Using GIS (A Case Study of the Lake Chad Basin). MSc. Thesis. University of Ibadan

Robertson, Campbell; Krauss, Clifford (2 August 2010). "Gulf Spill Is the Largest of Its Kind, Scientists Say". The New York Times. USA
\
Sahagun, Louis (2014). "Toxins released by oil spills send fish hearts into cardiac arrest". Los Angeles Times.USA

Sam How (1988). "After 10 Years, the Trauma of Love Canal Continues", New York Times. Retrieved 2008-07

SCOPE 5 (1979) Environmental Impact Assessment, 2nd Edition
Serle, W., Morel, G. J. & Hartwig, W. (1977). A Field Guide to the Birds of West Africa, London: Collins

Sky Truth (2010) ab"BP / Gulf Oil Spill – 68,000 Square Miles of Direct Impact" SkyTruth. (Press release).

The Department of the Environment (2010), The Environment Protection and Biodiversity Conservation Act, Australia: Water, Heritage and the Arts

The Brundlant Commission Report (2007), Our Common Future. Report of the World Commission on Environment(WCED). United Nations. USA

Tunnell W, Jr., Fabio Moretzsohn, and Jorge Brenner (May 2010). "Biodiversity of the Gulf of Mexico: Applications to the Deep Horizon oil spill" (Press release). Harte Research Institute for Gulf of Mexico Studies, Texas A&M University. Retrieved 14 June 2010

U.S Department of Agriculture, Soil Conservation Service (1997). Guides for Environmental Assessment,

U.S. Department of Agriculture, Natural Resources Conservation (1995). Environmental Effects of Resource Management Plan

U.S. Environmental Protection Agency (2002). Guideline on Choosing a Sampling Design for Environmental Data Collection for use in Developing a Quality Assurance Plan. EPA QA/G-5S

United Nations Environment Programme (1996) Environmental Impact Assessment – Basic Procedures for Developing Countries

United Nations Environment Programme (1987). The State of the World Environment, UNEP/GC

United States Environmental Protection Agency (2002). Guideline on Choosing Sampling Design for Environmental Data Collection, Office of Environmental Information, Washington DC

Vision 2010 Report (1997): Ecology and the Nigerian Environment. Federal Government of Nigeria

Wang, Alex (2007). "Environmental protection in China: the role of law"

Wathern P (1988). Environmental Impact Assessment: Theory and Practice. Unwin Hyema, London

Watson, Michael (2003). "Environmental Impact Assessment and European Community Law". XIV International Conference "Danube-River of Cooperation

Williamson, David (2003). "Exxon Valdez oil spill effects lasting far longer than expected, scientists say". University of North Carolina at Chapel Hill USA

Wines, Michael (2014). "Fish Embryos Exposed to Oil From BP Spill Develop Deformities, a Study Finds". The New York Times. USA

World Bank (1995). Environmental Assessment Source Book Updates. Environmental Auditing, Washington DC: The World Bank.

World Bank (1996). Environmental Assessment Sourcebook Volume I: Policies, Procedures and Cross-Sectoral Issues. World Bank Technical Paper No 139. The World Bank, Washington DC

World Bank (1996). Environmental Assessment Sourcebook Volume II: Sectoral Guidelines, World Bank Technical Paper No 140. The World Bank, Washington DC

World Bank (1996). Environmental Assessment Sourcebook Volume III: Guidelines for Environmental Assessment of Energy and Industry Projects. World Bank Technical Paper No 154. The World Bank, Washington DC

World Bank (1999) Environmental Assessment Source Book Updates, The World Bank. Washington DC

World Bank (1999). Pollution Prevention and Abatement Handbook: Towards Cleaner Production, Washington DC: The World Bank Group,

ABOUT THE AUTHOR

For many years, Benard Omoyeni has been one of the leading experts on Environmental Assessment and Management. He works as an Environmental Specialist in the oil and gas industry and has successfully pioneered different Environmental Studies for projects and operations in the industry. He has become phenomenal as Environmental Assessment Subject Matter Expert (SME).

From his wealth of experience and academic prowess, he has specifically been a Project Manager for over fifteen (15) Environmental Impact Assessment (EIA) projects and has continued to provide his wealth of experience in carrying out world class studies in this field. He has many publications to his credit in the research and academic journals.

Bernard has served as Lecturer in the Federal College of Freshwater Fisheries Technology, Baga, Borno State where he held increasingly different responsibilities which include: Head of Academics, Head of Fish Biology and Director of Studies between 1999 – 2005. He was involved in different research endeavors on the fisheries, ecology and environmental functioning at the college.

Benard obtained a Bachelor of Technology (B.Tech) in Fisheries and Wildlife from the University of Technology, Akure (1997); a Master of Public Administration (MPA) from the University of Maiduguri (2000-2001); a Master of Science (MSc) in Environmental Management (MEM) and Geographic Information System (GIS) at the University of Agriculture, Abeokuta (2003-2004) and University of Ibadan, (2004 -2005) respectively. He has membership with local and international professional bodies, notably: the Fisheries Society of Nigeria (FSN), Nigeria Environmental Society (NES), American Society of Safety Engineer (ASSE), Institute of Environmental Management and Assessment (IEMA). He has attended different trainings, seminars and workshops both locally and internationally.

He is married to Uzoma Omoyeni and their union is blessed with three great children: Newdawn, Delight and Excel Omoyeni

Printed in Great Britain
by Amazon

63359566R00157